Perspectives in European History

No. 1
THE MEDIEVAL MISSIONARY

THE MEDIEVAL MISSIONARY

A Study of the Conversion of Northern Europe
A.D. 500 – 1300

By

JAMES THAYER ADDISON

Professor of the History of Religion and Missions
Episcopal Theological School, Cambridge,
Massachusetts

PORCUPINE PRESS

Philadelphia 1976

First edition 1936
(New York: International Missionary Council.
Studies in the World Mission of Christianity
No. II, 1936)

Reprinted 1976 by
PORCUPINE PRESS, INC.
Philadelphia, Pennsylvania 19107

Library of Congress Cataloging in Publication Data

Addison, James Thayer, 1887-1953.
    The medieval missionary.

    (Perspectives in European history ; no. 1)
    Reprint of the 1936 ed. published by International
Missionary Council, New York, as no. 2 of Studies in
the world mission of Christianity.
    Bibliography: p.
    Includes index.
    1. Missions—History. 2. Missions—Europe.
3. Europe—Church history. 4. Church history—
Middle Ages, 600-1500. I. Title. II. Series:
Studies in the world mission of Christianity ; no. 2.
BV2110.A4   1976   266'.2'4   76-7628
ISBN 0-87991-610-9

Manufactured in the United States of America

To

THE DEAN AND FACULTY

OF

THE EPISCOPAL THEOLOGICAL SCHOOL

FOREWORD

It is a pleasure to be able to have, as the second number of these occasional *Studies*, this important monograph by Professor Addison. We have long stood in need of a thorough and comprehensive account of the conversion of the peoples of Western Europe. Of the previous narratives, G. F. Maclear, *A History of Christian Missions in The Middle Ages* (Cambridge and London, Macmillan and Co., 1863), while excellent in its day, has become badly out of date because of the immense amount of research in various aspects of the field in the past seventy years. A later book, C. H. Robinson, *The Conversion of Europe* (London, Longmans Green and Co., 1917) is a remarkable achievement for a busy editor and executive, but it is based upon only a fraction of the important sources and pertinent literature and in places is both inaccurate and superficial. The admirable long chapter on medieval missions by Moreau in Descamps, *Histoire Générale Comparée des Missions* (Paris, Libraire Plan, 1932) is of necessity only a summary, as are the pertinent sections in Schmidlin, *Katholische Missionsgeschichte* (Steyl, Missionsdruckerei, 1924), in its English edition by Braun, *Catholic Mission History* (Techny, Mission Press, S. V. D., 1933).

Professor Addison has spent a large part of several years in reading the sources and the many books and articles which deal with particular phases of the field. The resulting study, relatively brief though it has had to be, is based upon the most painstaking and comprehensive research. Here is a unique and important work, one which can be depended upon for its accuracy. Its modesty and its self-denying forswearal of numerous footnotes and other outward trappings of scholarship sometimes fail to disclose the really prodigious amount of labor which has gone into it and the exact scholarship of which it is the condensed summary. The self-imposed labor of love has been thoroughly and ably performed.

The book, too, has been well worth the doing. Through it we can now see the modern missionary enterprise against the background and from the perspective of the missions of earlier centuries. Between the missions of which Professor Addison writes and those of the last century and a half many striking contrasts exist which inevitably raise questions concerning the infallibility of those which have been pursued in our age.

The missions of which Professor Addison tells were staffed predominantly by men. They were often financed by the state. Frequently what was called conversion was brought about by force, often as a feature of the imperialistic program of a dominant race or ruling house, and more than once as an instrument through which an able and ambitious ruler extended his authority over his people and built a monarchy. The main object of missions was the conversion of non-Christians and the creation of a Christian Church. Conversions were usually *en masse*, with the minimum of preliminary instruction, and repeatedly with very little education subsequent to baptism. The prince often led the way and encouraged or commanded his subjects to follow. It was by the natural groupings of tribes and nations that the peoples of Western Europe came into the Church. It was centuries before any but a few had more than an inkling of the inward significance of the Christian faith. For the majority Christianity was a powerful and magical force through which miracles were wrought to the temporal advantage of the faithful and the skillful and by which hell was avoided and heaven attained. The missionaries were usually monks and it was generally assumed that there were two types of Christianity — the perfect exemplified in the monastic ideal and a secondary and less exacting but permissible kind for the large majority of Christians. Usually within a generation missionaries ceased to have much voice in the churches they had founded. The clergy quickly became predominantly native and, save for the supervision exercised from Rome and except in some places where the subject majority were exploited politically and for the economic profit of a ruling race, the control of the church soon passed into the hands of what we term today the "indigenous" clergy and laity. The Christianity and the culture of modern Europe still display characteristics which are the results of these methods.

On the other hand, the missions of the past century and a half, and especially those maintained by Protestants, have been and are different from those of which Professor Addison writes. The large majority of missionaries are now not men but women. Missions are seldom financed by the state, except in the indirect form of subsidies to schools and hospitals which as a rule are given irrespective of the religious complexion of the institution aided. In contrast, missions are supported by missionary societies which derive their income from the voluntary gifts of millions of donors. Force has been infrequently applied to bring about acceptance of baptism — although the display of force has often contributed to the outward respect paid the missionary. More and more, indeed, the Christian conscience protests against the use of violence against backward peoples and in the supposed interest of missions. Mass conversions have been seen, but they have not been the rule and, when they have occurred, have often come in spite of the missionary rather than through any deliberate plans made by him. The missionary, and especially the Protestant missionary, has sought to win individuals one by one. To be sure, Protestant missionaries have sought the conversion of the natural leaders, hoping that through these the masses might be reached. As a result of these methods, some outstanding Christians have emerged, but more often than not the masses have not followed them into the Church. Their influence on the majority of their fellow-countrymen, rather, has been exerted through reforms in the political or educational structure of the group or the nation. Except among primitive peoples or depressed classes, only a relatively few thousands of converts have been made. The great majority of the peoples to whom nineteenth and twentieth century Protestant missionaries have gone have ostensibly remained non-Christian. In many instances, however, their ideals and customs have been profoundly modified by contact with Christianity and the non-Christian religious systems have paid Christianity the sincere flattery of imitation. A type of mass conversion has occurred in such lands as India, China, and Japan. However, it has not been registered by baptism or by admission to the Church, but by some degree of conformity to the ethical and spiritual standards of Christianity. Much more emphasis is placed on schools, hospitals, and various benevolent enterprises for non-Christians which have as their effect the leavening of an entire culture rather than conversion than was ever dreamed of in the Middle Ages. For those who have sought admission to the Church both Roman Catholic and Protestant missionaries have in practice set much more exacting standards of instruction, either before or after baptism, or both, than was the rule in Medieval Europe. Two ideals of Christian living are no longer acknowledged. All are encouraged to live up to the full demands of the New Testament. For entrance into the Church much more is made of the work of the Spirit in effecting a new birth and an inward transformation. Moreover, the younger churches planted by missionaries remain much longer dependent upon foreign funds and personnel than was true in Medieval Europe, and that in spite of the slogan which calls for self-supporting, self-governing, and self-propagating churches. Yet before we say that in this respect the missions of the present have failed, we need to remind ourselves that in many great lands Protestant missions are only one, two, or three generations old, while the span of time which Professor Addison is covering is approximately a thousand years.

We must not quickly conclude that the methods employed in the conversion of Europe can be made to work today. The peoples among whom they were used were not far removed from a primitive stage of civilization and were confined to a comparatively small portion of the earth's surface. If applicable at all, the medieval methods would probably be

successful chiefly among such peoples of primitive culture as
are to be found in Africa, and in the hills of Burma, India,
and Southern and Western China, or as are the depressed
classes of India. Yet the reading of Professor Addison's
excellent pages cannot but prove thought provoking to every
serious student of modern missions.

KENNETH SCOTT LATOURETTE.

Yale University, 1936.

PREFACE

THE main facts relating to the spread of Christianity in northern Europe and the conversion of its peoples are to be found in the pages of general histories. In greater detail parts of the story have been written in more specialized works concerned with particular periods or individual leaders. But, with the exception of a few German and French monographs of very limited scope, reliable material for medieval missionary history is scattered in hundreds of different books — in general history, in church history, or in biography — and even where found, it is seldom treated from the point of view of those whose primary interest is in missions, — their motive, their technique, and their evolution. To assemble and to unify this scattered material is the purpose of this volume.

What I have here attempted is to treat only certain obvious factors of outstanding importance — the influence of rulers, the influence of monasteries, and the influence of the papacy. The forces directly operating to attain the formal conversion of any people and the events leading up to that achievement supply my subject matter. A further field for study into which I have scarcely entered is no doubt of equal value and interest — the result of this formal conversion, the effect upon the moral and social life of the people, the inter-action of old and new religious beliefs and practices, and, in the light of these later developments, the appraisal of the missionary methods employed. This large subject, so difficult to define and to isolate, deserves a treatment fuller than it has ever received and more skilful than I am able to give it.

I have included in my survey most of the important material from the sixth to the thirteenth century in Scotland, England, Holland, Germany, and Scandinavia; and because this material is presented not by countries but by topics some degree of repetition has occasionally been required, not too great, I hope, for the reader to pardon. In covering so wide an area over so long a stretch of time it has been necessary to lean heavily upon the work of others, though I have tried to make full use of the primary sources. The bibliography records my indebtedness and indicates the full range of the material examined, while the "Suggestions for Further Reading" provide a brief list of more easily available books, chiefly in English.

J. T. A.

Episcopal Theological School,
Cambridge, Massachusetts.

Acknowledgments

The author wishes to acknowledge gratefully the courtesy of the following publishers and authors for permission to use the quotations taken from the books listed below:

The American-Scandinavian Foundation (New York): A. Olrik, *Viking Civilization;* G. Bell & Sons (London): A. M. Sellar, translation of Bede's *Ecclesiastical History of England;* Chatto & Windus (London): E. Kylie, *English Correspondence of St. Boniface;* Harvard University Press (Cambridge): J. E. King, Bede's *Ecclesiastical History* (translated by King in Loeb Classical Library); G. W. Robinson, *Willibald's Life of Boniface;* W. Heffer & Sons (Cambridge, England): E. Monsen, translation of Snorre Sturlason's *Heimskringla;* S. Kiek, Doran & Co., Ltd. (London): A. Plummer, *Churches in Britain before A.D. 1000;* Longmans Green & Co., Ltd. (London): C. H. Robinson, *Conversion of Europe;* The Society for Promoting Christian Knowledge (London): G. F. Browne, *Boniface of Crediton;* C. H. Robinson, *The Life of Otto;* The Society for the Propagation of the Gospel in Foreign Parts (London): A. Grieve, *Willibrord;* C. H. Robinson, *Life of Anskar.*

J. T. A.

CONTENTS

THE MEDIEVAL MISSIONARY

CHAPTER I

THE EDUCATION AND THE MOTIVES OF MEDIEVAL MISSIONARIES

THE men who labored to Christianize the peoples of northern Europe during the early Middle Ages are little known to the average reader of history. A few, like Boniface in Germany, Augustine of Canterbury, and perhaps Columba of Iona, are familiar figures in the pages of secular history; but most of them enjoy no general fame. The conditions, moreover, under which they worked were so different from those which surrounded the missionaries of earlier and of later times that their methods are equally unfamiliar. In an era when the religion of the ruler determined the religion of his people, when the power of the papacy was increasing, and when monasteries were the stimulating centers of education and of religious zeal, missionary activity was inevitably guided and controlled by these factors. None of them was present in the first centuries of Christian expansion and none exists today in its original strength. For that reason the methods of medieval missions, taken as a whole, are in a class by themselves; and whether for purposes of historical research or with the more practical aim of learning from the mistakes and the achievements which characterize them, they are worthy of study.

To consider first the education of these medieval missionaries and the motives which inspired them will serve to introduce us to the men themselves and to give us at least a slight acquaintance with the personalities of the leaders whose methods we are to investigate.

Of the many missionaries responsible for the conversion of Scotland after 500, by far the best known is Columba.[1] Born in Donegal in 521, he had studied, before the age of

[1] The *Life of Columba* was written by Adamnan probably between 692 and 697. Adamnan (624–704), the ninth abbot of Iona, had had frequent opportunity in his boyhood to converse with those who had seen Columba and had before him an earlier *Life* by Cummene the Fair.

twenty-three, at the monastery of Moville under Finnian, in Leinster under the bard Gemman, and later at the monasteries of Clonard and Glasnevin. During the next nineteen years he was active as a missionary organizer in various parts of Ireland, founding his chief monasteries at Derry and at Durrow, as well as others elsewhere. His preparation, both academic and practical, was thus both long and thorough, and he did not begin what we should call foreign missionary work until the age of forty-two.

Though the education of Columba can be thus briefly described, the mixed motives which prompted him to undertake his mission to Scotland are not so easy to determine. That he should abandon at the age of forty-two the career of an ascetic missionary in Ireland was probably due to a clan quarrel in which he was embroiled and which led to public disfavor. In selecting the borderland of Scottish Dalriada as his field of work he may well have been guided by sympathy with his racial kinsmen there and the desire to aid their cause by means both political and religious. In short, his reasons for leaving Ireland and entering Scotland were directly connected with political events. Yet his religious motives were undoubtedly fundamental. As his biographer Adamnan puts it, "he desired to go on pilgrimage for the sake of Christ," a phrase which indicates the deepest motive of most of the medieval Irish missionaries. They were characteristically ascetics on pilgrimage rather than missionaries on business. That is, their central aim was to lead a life of seclusion and austerity. Not evangelism but asceticism was the keynote of their careers.

Of the missionaries to whom we owe the conversion of the seven kingdoms of seventh-century England we do not know enough to analyze their motives, but it is clear that a thorough education in monasteries and monastic schools was the preparation for their work of evangelism.[2] Augustine and those who accompanied him to Kent in 596 came from the monas-

[2] The great source for a study of the conversion of the Saxon Kingdoms is Bede's *Ecclesiastical History*. See Bibliography.

tery of St. Andrew's in Rome. Mellitus, Justus, Paulinus, and Rufinianus, who came in 601, had had the same training. Aidan, Cedd, Diuma, Ceollach, Trumhne, Jaruman, Fursa, Chad, and Wilfrid, whom we associate with the other kingdoms, received their education at Lindisfarne, at Iona, or in Irish monasteries. Agilbert, too, had spent years of study in Ireland. Felix was probably the product of one of the monasteries of Columbanus in Burgundy. Of the previous schooling of James the Deacon, Birinus, and Wini we are not told; but it is a sound assumption that they, too, had known monastic training.

The earliest important missionary on the Continent in the sixth century was Columban, or Columbanus, whose personality has been made real to us through his famous Life by the monk Jonas.[3] Columban was born in western Leinster in the district lying between Louth and southern Lough Erne. The year of his birth is quite uncertain but may be placed with some probability between 540 and 543. After attending some monastic or lay school in his vicinity, he went next to a school under the abbot Sinell who had recently founded a monastery on Cleenish Island (Cluain-Inis) in Lough Erne. There, as his biographer tells us, he "sweated" with the greatest zeal in the study of grammar, rhetoric, geometry, and the Holy Scriptures. After a long period with Sinell, Columban entered the new monastery of Bangor (in Ulster) which had been founded in 558 by the famous Comgall. There he obtained what may be soberly described as the best education then available in Western Europe. The one central subject pursued for its own sake was the Scriptures, of which Columban always showed a masterly grasp and from which he constantly quotes in his letters. His keen interest in biblical study — even after he had begun work in the wilds of the Vosges mountains — is revealed in a letter to Pope Gregory I (c. 595–600) in which Columban says, "I have read your work on the *Pastoral Office* . . . I hear you have written

[3] The *Vita Columbani* by the monk Jonas is one of the most important historical documents of the seventh century. It was written about 642, only twenty-seven years after Columban's death.

two wonderful little books of homilies on the prophet Ezekiel; send them to me, I beseech you, for I am thirsting to read them. I have read the six books of St. Jerome on this prophet, but they do not cover even half the ground. Therefore send us at least your second book on Ezekiel, as well as a commentary on the Song of Songs . . . and elucidate for us the obscurities of the prophecy of Zechariah."[4]

With this study of the Bible went, of course, a generally correct knowledge of Latin, and in the case of Columban an acquaintance with prosody and the ability to write Latin verse. As auxiliary subjects the monks likewise read the more celebrated western Fathers, especially Jerome, and a certain number of non-Christian Latin authors. Indeed, there are traces in Columban's poems and letters of familiarity with Virgil, Ovid, Horace, Sallust, Persius, and others.

Since Columban did not leave Bangor on his mission to the Frankish Kingdom until he was over forty-five years old (c. 589), his period of training was longer than that enjoyed by most of the early medieval missionaries. He set out upon his life's work not as a novice but as a leader of long experience and wide learning.

Like nearly all the Irish monks who emigrated to the continent in the early Middle Ages, Columban was not primarily a missionary to the heathen. He seems never to have deliberately planned to work among pagans of his own accord and for their sake. The two accounts we possess of his original motives support this conclusion and are in harmony with all that we know of other Irish monks who followed his example. His biographer Jonas tells us that after he had been for many years in the monastery at Bangor he began to feel the longing for *peregrinatio*, "mindful of the command of the Lord to Abraham, 'Get thee out of thy country, and from thy kindred, and from thy father's house, and go into a land which I shall show thee'." This longing to "travel abroad," which moved nearly all these Irish monks to cross to Britain or the continent, was a combination of a purely

[4] Epistle 1. *M. G. H. Epistolae*, vol. III.

human *Wanderlust* with a zealous desire to extend the limits of asceticism to the point of renouncing not only family life and worldly possessions but even fatherland and the comforting companionship of their monastic community. It meant laying just that much more of value as a sacrifice on the altar of the Lord. The aim was to depart into unknown wilds, forsaking all. Whether those wilds were in a country that might be described as Christian or in one known still to be pagan was a matter of accident or of indifference, for in a sense not ignoble the *peregrinus* was much more concerned to save his own soul than to save the souls of others.

Though he wrote more than two hundred years after Columban's death, Walahfrid Strabo, the biographer of Columban's companion Gall, gives the true interpretation of those motives which had been familiar to him in hundreds of other cases. "St. Columban," he tells us, "earnestly desiring to attain that perfection spoken of in the Gospel — namely, to leave all he had, take up his cross and follow the Lord, stripped of all possessions — succeeded in persuading those of his brethren whose souls were inflamed with a like fervor, to make good their zeal by action, by renouncing the sweets of kindred and home."[5]

Obedient to this motive Columban crossed from Ireland to Brittany with twelve companions. There they determined "to make earnest enquiry into the character and behavior of the people, that they might remain longer if they found they could sow the seeds of salvation; or in case they found the people's minds hardened by the darkness of an arrogant pride, they might press on to the neighboring nations." And by "neighboring nations" they did not mean the pagan tribes of Germany but the people of Christian Italy. This seems a fair inference from the fact that twenty years later, after being driven from his monasteries in Burgundy, Columban asked Chlotar II of Neustria to aid him in making the journey over the Alps to Italy. It was only at the earnest

[5] Walahfrid, I, c. 2. Joynt's translation.

request of Theodebert of Austrasia that he consented to remain in the latter's dominions. He then established himself at Bregenz on Lake Constance where the people appear to have been a mixture of lapsed Christians and pure pagans. Once during this period he seems to have contemplated a mission to the heathen Wends, but a contrary vision intervened, and nothing came of the plan. Finally, after Theodebert's death, when Columban felt it necessary to leave Bregenz, it was to Christian Italy that he went and in Italy that he died.

The earliest Anglo-Saxon missionary to make a permanent impression upon a continental field was Willibrord, who devoted his life to evangelization in what is now Holland.[6] He was born in Northumbria of Anglian parents in 657 or 658. His father Wilgils, "as soon as the infant was weaned, entrusted him to the brothers of the church at Ripon," the monastery of which the famous Wilfrid of York became abbot about 660. It was in 678 that Wilfrid was driven from his see by King Egfrid and went overseas to Rome, an incident that may well have created trouble in the monastery at Ripon. At any rate, it was in that year, when he was twenty years old, that Willibrord left Ripon, and, attracted by the fame of Irish learning and the reputation of the monastic leader Egbert, went to his monastery in Ireland, where he studied for the next twelve years. Before setting out upon his missionary career in 690 Willibrord had thus reached the age of thirty-two, having spent at least twenty-five years of study and training in two of the most famous monasteries of the time.

It is not difficult to discover the stimulus which prompted Willibrord to undertake a missionary career in Frisia. His first monastic master had been Wilfrid at Ripon; the leader under whom he studied in Ireland was Egbert; and among Egbert's other followers was Wigbert. All three of these men were successively identified with missionary work in Frisia. Wilfrid, driven from his see of York by King Egfrid

---

[6] Our chief source for the life of Willibrord is Alcuin's *Vita Willibrordi*.

early in 678, landed in Frisia and spent that winter, under the patronage of King Aldgisl, in missionary labor. Subsequently, at an unknown date prior to 690, Egbert made an abortive attempt to reach Frisia, and Wigbert, one of his fellow monks, preached there for two years. Three of the men, therefore, to whom Willibrord had chiefly looked for guidance from earliest youth had set him an example of missionary zeal, and, according to Bede, Egbert was definitely responsible for sending Willibrord to Frisia. When we add to this line of succession the more notable name of Boniface, who began his labors in Frisia and later worked for two years with Willibrord, we have an interesting example of the extent to which, in all periods of missionary history, the torch of enthusiasm has been handed on from leader to leader.

If such was the stimulus which roused the missionary motive of Willibrord, the motive itself is hardly less in doubt. It was plainly the simple desire to preach the Gospel among the heathen. Willibrord, like Boniface, did not set forth primarily as a pilgrim nor as an anchorite. From the beginning he concentrated, so far as circumstances permitted, upon the work of conversion.

Wynfrith, the future Boniface, was born in southwestern Wessex shortly before 675.[7] His father was a Christian Saxon, a landholder of noble blood. At some time during his boyhood he was placed by his father in a monastery at Ad-Escancastre, the modern Exeter. But the lack of competent teachers of reading at Exeter determined him, after some years, to seek a monastery where higher scholastic standards prevailed. He therefore moved to the Benedictine monastery at Nhutscelle [8] where Winbert was abbot. It is to this same famous abbot that Boniface later referred as "Winbert, of revered memory, once my abbot and master." Under the leadership of Winbert, Nhutscelle was a seat of literary culture, and afforded opportunities for varied and thorough

[7] The earliest and most reliable Life of Boniface is that by Willibald. Our other chief source is found in his letters. *S. Bonifatii et Lulli Epistolae.* See Bibliography.

[8] The modern Nursling or Nutshalling between Winchester and Southampton.

study of which Boniface took full advantage. If he had been content to be merely a monk he would not have left Ad-Escancastre; but in his new surroundings he engaged in the devoted pursuit not only of grammar and metrics but above all of the Scriptures and biblical exegesis. How completely Boniface mastered the arts of grammar and metrics we learn from the fact that he wrote a text-book on grammar and that he frequently introduced verses of his own composition not only in letters to his friends but even in a letter to Pope Zacharias. The range and depth of his biblical knowledge was notable both during his days at Nhutscelle and throughout his later life. In the monastery he became a teacher of exegesis widely known for his scholarship and spiritual power, and in numerous letters composed in his maturity and old age there is abundant evidence of a mind saturated with scriptural lore. In addition to innumerable quotations and allusions there are frequent references to Boniface's continuous study of the Bible, as when he writes in 735 to the Abbess Eadburga of Thanet asking for a copy of St. Peter's epistles and to Abbot Dud telling him that he has commentaries on Romans and I. Corinthians but that he desires other commentaries on St. Paul which he lacks.

The recognition accorded to his unusual capacity as scholar and teacher is reflected in his ordination as priest soon after the age of thirty, for at that period few monks were ordained to the priesthood, and only such as were above the average in learning and holiness. Further testimony to the cultural opportunities of Boniface and his zeal in making the most of them appears from the influence upon him of Aldhelm, Abbot of Malmesbury and one of the most brilliant and learned Englishmen of the day. A letter from Aedilwald (Ethelwald) to Aldhelm speaks of "Wynfrith, my client and thine" and of Wynfrith's "journey across the sea," and it is altogether probable that the author was the future king Ethelwald of Mercia (716–757) and the Wynfrith was Boniface himself. That Boniface had long been indebted to Aldhelm as a literary and intellectual master is likewise

plain from the clear traces of the abbot's influence in Boniface's earlier thought and style.

Before beginning his independent career as a missionary
Boniface was to supplement his years of cloistered study with
practical experience in the ecclesiastical world of his time.
According to Willibald, "in the reign of Ine, King of the West
Saxons, a sudden emergency impended upon the rise of a
new dissension; and immediately the chief men of the
churches, with the advice of King Ine, summoned a council
of the servants of God. And presently, when all were assembled, a most healthful discussion concerning this recent
dissension wisely arose among the priestly ranks of the ecclesiastical order. And . . . they decided to send trusty
legates in the Lord to the archbishop of the city of Canterbury, Bertwald by name. . . . Immediately the king addressed all the servants of Christ, asking whom they would
charge with the message of this embassy." [9] In response to
his question Abbot Winbert of Nhutscelle, Abbot Wintra of
Tisbury, and Abbot Beorwald of Glastonbury, together
with other leaders, united in naming Boniface as the chief of
an embassy from Wessex to Canterbury. Though we have
no means of knowing the exact date, it must have been
between 692 and 712. As to the cause in question many
possible conjectures have been made but none convincing
to the scientific historian. From the point of view of Boniface's reputation and education, however, the important
point is that he was chosen for a mission of great responsibility, that he executed it successfully, and that "his name
was so spread abroad and was held in such honor, not only
among all lay authorities but also among all ranks of the
ecclesiastical service, that from that time he advanced more
and more, and very often took part in their synodal assembly." [9]

We are fully justified in concluding that Boniface's experience in this task and in the wider fields of service to
which it led gave him ample opportunity to test and to in-

[9] Willibald, c. 4. Robinson's translation.

crease his practical ability in spheres outside of the cloister and won him the friendship, so valuable to him in later life, of Archbishop Bertwald and of many of the metropolitan clergy. At the threshold of his career abroad there was every indication that a notable career awaited him at home.

But before leaving England for the last time as the future Apostle of Germany, Boniface went through a further period of training, this time as a missionary in the field. Having obtained with some difficulty the consent and support of Abbot Winbert, he set forth in 716 with two or three other monks for the heathen country of Frisia. But after less than a year and a half of labors in that disturbed region, a successful rebellion of the pagan King Radbod against his overlord Charles Martel created such havoc in the weak Christian community that Boniface and his brethren thought it the part of wisdom to return to England.

Soon after his arrival at Nhutscelle Abbot Winbert died, and Boniface was unanimously chosen to succeed him. Still determined, however, to resume the work of a missionary, Boniface declined the election, and late in the same year (718) set out for Rome. By the end of 719 he was back again in Frisia, there to serve for over two years under the guidance of Archbishop Willibrord, his Saxon predecessor in that difficult field. Here Boniface could study and practise the technique and method of missionary evangelism and the care and nurture of infant churches; and to this long drill in a hard school the future achievements of Boniface owed much.

No man of more distinguished ability than Boniface has ever undertaken the work of foreign missions, and no man has ever entered the field as a leader after a preparation quite so thorough and complete. Before leaving England for the first time he had studied and taught in monasteries for some thirty-five years, absorbing and mastering the best learning of his day; and for perhaps eight or ten years of that time he had taken an active part in the ecclesiastical life of Wessex. Not until he was forty or forty-one did he begin his years of apprenticeship in the practical work of missions, and not until he was forty-seven did he assume leadership as a bishop in Germany. From the outset of his career he could count upon the advantage not only of natural endowment and of powerful support but of prolonged and richly varied education.

As an Anglo-Saxon monk of the eighth century Boniface shared the temper of his race, his profession, and his age. We find in him that readiness for adventure and that eagerness to overcome difficulties which produce and sustain the spirit of the pioneer. And in him, as a Christian monk, that impulse was mastered by a profound religious faith and enlisted in the service of the Church. His vigorous manhood demanded a strenuous life and his chosen vocation determined its setting and its direction. More than that, the custom of his time and the habits of its thought made it natural that he should find an outlet for this active religious devotion in distant and dangerous parts, where, in conformity with the monastic ideal, he could literally and physically forsake his friends and relatives and country for the sake of the Lord. Only so could all his strongest impulses find their satisfaction through "enduring hardness as a good soldier of Jesus Christ."

As was the case with hundreds of others, these desires and purposes would have been sufficient to make him a missionary even though he had felt but slightly the primary missionary motive — the longing to convert the heathen. For in most of the Celtic missionaries and in certain of the Anglo-Saxon that strict and definite motive for evangelism was wanting. Their activity in conversion was really a by-product of their lives as monastic exiles and pilgrims. But there is ample evidence that Boniface was stirred from beginning to end by the passionate longing to win pagans to the knowledge of Christ and to saving membership in his Church. With him the pursuit of that enterprise was not incidental but central.

He began his career abroad, as we have seen, by a missionary expedition to the heathen Frisians and gave it up for the time being only because the condition of the country forbade successful work. Within a year of his return "he strove with the utmost solicitude to renew and repeat the journey which he had laid aside." So strong was his intent that he declined election as abbot of Nhutscelle and so persistent was his refusal that Bishop Daniel of Winchester was finally obliged to provide the monastery with another abbot.

After receiving from the Pope in 719 a commission "to inspect the savage peoples of Germany," he returned to pagan Frisia and labored under Willibrord for about two years until an offer to succeed his bishop reminded him that the field appointed by the Pope still awaited him. Thenceforward until just before his death his activities combined those of an evangelist among heathen and a reforming organizer among Christian and half-Christian peoples in Germany and the Frankish kingdom. Yet we cannot but feel that, broadly speaking, it was the Popes who were responsible for his work as reformer and organizer and that his own inmost desires and hopes centred about his work as an evangelist. It is true, of course, that his obedience to papal commands and purposes was essentially a glad and ready obedience and that the great ecclesiastical tasks assigned to him were in keeping with his capacities. So far from being a discontented misfit in the rôle that had been thrust upon him, he could not have failed to realize that the labor of building in semi-Christian lands was a necessary complement to the task of direct evangelism; and his administrative powers grew and strengthened under the weight of responsibility.

At the same time, however, there are signs that the part of pioneer was the more congenial to him and that more than once he would gladly have returned to it, had it not been for the exacting plans of his chief at Rome. He tried, while at Rome in 737–8, to win release from ecclesiastical duties in Hesse and Thuringia which had by then been formally Christianized; but the Pope declined to let him go. It is more than probable that the field which Boniface had in mind was the territory of the Saxons, for just at this time he had been writing to the clergy and people of England begging for their prayers so that God might "turn to the Catholic faith the hearts of the pagan Saxons." "Have pity on them," he pleads, "because even they themselves are wont to say 'We are of one blood and of one bone' . . . act now upon this our appeal." And this same zealous desire of Boniface is recognized in a letter from the Bishop of Leicester who wrote him, "Protected by God's right hand, you meditate night and day, that the hearts of the pagan Saxons may be turned to the Catholic and apostolic faith." [10] For pressing outward into Saxon territory he had, in addition to the normal missionary motive, the statesman's motive to protect his Christians in Hesse and Thuringia, because as long as the Saxons remained heathen their Christian neighbors were in constant danger not only of attack but of relapse.

If this evidence of the motives of Boniface at the height of his career is not wholly convincing, it is at least congruous with the beginning of that career and with its close. Indeed, the end of the saint's life affords us the most moving testimony to his unspent missionary ardor. When over seventy years old he resigned the archbishopric of Mainz. With every sign about him to encourage the belief that his life's work was ended, with achievements behind him sufficient to make him one of the great figures of the Middle Ages, and with the prospect before him of a peaceful withdrawal to his beloved monastery of Fulda, he turned his back on comforts and rewards and the security of honored retirement, and set his face steadfastly toward the distant borders of Frisia. When at last he was free, when he had discharged every duty laid upon him by the Church and had won the right to end his days in accordance with his heart's desire, he became once more the pioneer, and met his death at the hands of pagans whom he had come to win.

Closely connected with that of Boniface is the career of Gregory of Utrecht. Born about 707 of a noble Frankish family, Gregory was educated at a school at the king's court

[10] Epistles 46, 47. Kylie's translation.

until he was about fifteen years old. After leaving school, he went to visit his grandmother Addula who was abbess of the convent at Pfalzel near Trèves, and while there he met Boniface who in that same year (722) was consecrated bishop. As the great missionary sat at table with the abbess and others, the boy Gregory was sent for and asked to read aloud to them from the Bible. When he had finished, Boniface said to him, "You read well, my son, if you understand what you read." Gregory declared that he did understand and, to prove it, repeated *verbatim* the passage in Latin which he had just read. Whereupon Boniface called upon him to translate it into the German vernacular, which Gregory confessed that he could not do. "Would you like to have me explain it to you?" enquired Boniface. And when Gregory assented, Boniface had him repeat the words slowly in Latin and then interpreted the passage in German to all who were present. Deeply impressed by this experience and by the personality of the saint, Gregory longed to attach himself to Boniface and told Addula that he wanted to go with Boniface and be his disciple. After refusing his plea many times, his grandmother finally yielded to his ardent persistence and consented to send him under escort to Boniface in Thuringia. Thenceforward until the death of Boniface in 754 Gregory remained his devoted companion, cherished as if he were an only son and sharing in all his master's arduous missionary labors.[11]

Gregory is a case, perhaps unique, of a famous missionary who began his career in the field of evangelism when no more than fifteen years old. Lacking any previous monastic preparation, he had the incomparable training afforded by constant personal association for some thirty years with the greatest missionary of the age.

Liudger, who wrote the Life of Gregory and later became Bishop of Münster, was a Frisian whose grandfather had been a friend of Willibrord. His parents sent him to Greg-

[11] The *Vita Gregorii* was written by Liudger, a pupil of Gregory's, very soon after the latter's death.

ory's monastic school at St. Martin's, Utrecht. After receiving his education there, he went to England to study under Alcuin at York where he was ordained deacon and remained for a year. A few years later he received permission from Gregory to go back to York for further study under Alcuin, with whom he stayed for three and a half years more before beginning his missionary career in Frisia. He thus had the privilege of prolonged study for some fifteen years under the two men who were probably the greatest teachers of their age.

In 801, eight years before the death of Liudger, Anskar, the Apostle of the North, was born. His birthplace was perhaps in Corbie, four miles from Amiens, perhaps further north in Flanders.[12] When he was about five years old his father sent him to school — undoubtedly the monastic school at Corbie. Probably in 813 he entered the monastery of Corbie, received the tonsure, and began to grow up under monastic teaching. In company with the monk Witmar he was subsequently placed in charge of the monastery's *schola exterior*, the school for outside children. Corbie, which had been founded in 662, was at this time one of the most important monasteries in the kingdom, already marked for its learning and its political influence.

After nine or ten years at Corbie Anskar was chosen for an important mission. In 816 Adalhard the Younger, then abbot of Corbie, had founded a branch monastery called New Corvey at Hetha in the Sollinger Wald. When this site proved unsatisfactory Adalhard arranged to transfer the monastery to Höxter on the right bank of the Weser, and in August, 822, the monks took possession of their new home. To aid them in reëstablishing and reviving New Corvey a picked group of monks was sent out soon afterwards from the mother monastery, and Anskar was numbered among them. There he served both as a teacher — the first master of the school—

---

[12] The *Vita Anskarii* was written soon after Anskar's death by his missionary companion Rimbert. It is highly rated by historians as probably the most reliable of medieval saints' lives and as one of the most important sources of the early Middle Ages.

and as a preacher to the people in church. It was some four years later (in 826) that he received and answered his first call to the mission field.

The preparation of Anskar for his missionary career was thus like that of many of his distinguished predecessors — an extensive training in one of the best monasteries of his time, begun at an early age and completed with honorable distinction. His record, however, is different in two respects from that of most other notable missionary leaders of the period. In the first place he began his evangelistic work at the age of twenty-five, far earlier than was usual. In the second place the last four years of his education, spent at a frontier post among the Saxons, provided the valuable experience of a kind of practical field work midway between civilization and paganism — a transition from the safe seclusion of Corbie to the wilds of Denmark.

We are given an occasional glimpse into the inner consciousness of Anskar when we read of the visions that he frequently experienced, several of which he related in full to his intimate friend and biographer Rimbert. At least two of these indicate that from an early age he was stirred by a purely missionary motive very rare among his fellow monks. Some years after he received the tonsure and presumably while he was still under twenty he had a prolonged vision near the close of which he beheld the majesty of God and heard a voice saying to him, "Go, and return to me crowned with martyrdom." And thereafter he began to prepare himself more seriously for the service of God in the hope that "he might be able to obtain the crown of martyrdom." Again, in another vision, which came to him just before his call to the Swedish mission (829), he beheld once more a light from heaven shining around him and heard a voice which said, "Go, and declare the word of God unto the nations." This experience, according to Rimbert, made him all the more readily eager to accept the summons to Sweden.

An inner call to give himself to the evangelization of pagan peoples marks Anskar as one of those who were not

missionaries by accident but who found in the conversion of
the heathen their dominant purpose in life.

One of the few remaining missionaries within our period
of whose preparation for work we have full knowledge is Otto,
Bishop of Bamberg.[13] Education is hardly the term to apply
to his varied experience before he set out to spend a few years
as the Apostle to Pomerania, for he was almost an old man
when he became a missionary. He was born in Swabia of a
noble family about the year 1060 and is reported to have
studied in his youth the rules of grammar and meter and the
works of certain Latin poets and philosophers. He never
became a learned man but was obviously well trained in
biblical studies and in all that pertained to church teaching.
Before he was thirty he went to the court of Duke Wladislav
of Poland as chaplain to the latter's wife Judith, who was
a sister of the Emperor Henry IV. There he not only learned
the language but also "fitted himself to take part in embassies
and in negotiations of various kinds with important persons."
After his return in 1090 Otto was charged by Henry IV with
superintending the erection of the cathedral at Speyer, and
when the emperor came back from Italy in 1097 Otto was
employed at court, becoming chancellor for some months in
1102 before his appointment at the close of that year to the
bishopric of Bamberg. By the time he undertook his first
mission to Pomerania in 1124 he had lived a full lifetime. He
entered upon his brief service in the mission field with an
ample equipment scarcely paralleled in missionary history,
bringing to bear upon his task the experience of a trained
diplomat and statesman, a practised organizer, and an aggressive ecclesiastical leader.

Otto was thus at least sixty years of age and had been
Bishop of Bamberg for twenty years before he undertook his
first mission to Pomerania. As one of the foremost ecclesiastics of Germany he was thoroughly at home in secular life
and in the best sense worldly wise. He was thus as far as

[13] There are three Lives of Otto, all written within twenty years of his death. The
greater part of those by Ebo and Herbordus is available in translation. See Bibliography.

possible from being a romantic ascetic of the *peregrinus* type. As a great organizer and a forceful leader he was loaned by his diocese for a year or two to perform a definite piece of work in founding the Church in Pomerania. Yet in his motives he plainly differed from many other ecclesiastics of this time and of the two preceding centuries. As the Church's dealings with the Wends in the eleventh and twelfth centuries showed, a grasping desire to extend political control and to increase the revenues of the Church was characteristic of much so-called missionary activity and largely accounted for its failure. But every stage of Otto's work proves that he was far more concerned with what he could give to the Pomeranians than with what he could get out of them. At heavy expense to himself in effort and money he established the Church over a wide area. Whether we accept the accounts of his biographers at their face value or prefer to read cautiously between the lines, we are impressed with the honesty of his character and the purity of his motives. His whole career in the field of his missionary labors substantiates what he is reported to have said to his trusted priest Udalric — "Although I have much urgent business both public and private in these parts [Bamberg], the love of Christ constrains me to attempt immediately the difficult task of going as a messenger to the Pomeranians, in order that I may spread the glory of His Name." [14]

[14] Ebo, II, 3.

CHAPTER II

KINGS AND MISSIONARIES

THE outstanding characteristic of medieval missions in northern Europe from A.D. 500 to 1200 is the prominent and decisive part played by rulers in the conversion of the people. Whether the chief was the ruler of a clan, a tribe, or a petty kingdom, his subjects were usually converted as subjects and not as individuals. Why such a type of conversion was natural in the circumstances is clear enough when we consider the social organization and the cultural level of the age. During the era of conversion the pagan peoples were under the domination of social and political systems in which the group controlled the individual. They felt and thought in terms of the clan or the tribe. And even when we give the name of kingdom to larger units, there still prevailed a group-consciousness of the tribal type. In such groups individualism was at a minimum and the will of the leader, embodying racial tradition, exerted a force almost unquestioned. Furthermore, the type of rudimentary nature-religion characteristic of this stage of culture was not an affair of individual conviction but of corporate loyalty. The religion was the religion of a group — the clan, the tribe, or the race. It was concerned with ritual observances of immemorial antiquity maintained for the purpose of promoting the material welfare of the social unit. It was therefore merely one aspect of the tribal life and shared the same corporate solidarity. Since it did not appeal to the individual as such, it was not to be questioned or abandoned by the individual acting alone. Its perpetuation or its supersession was a tribal matter, an affair of State. No single man could work by himself; the people must move together or not at all. So it was that in European history of this period the king or some lesser lord, acting in his representative capacity, was usually the first to move. Even when the ensuing procedure, as in Norway, was in accordance with democratic forms, the leadership was necessarily royal and the whole process moved from the top down.

Examples are so numerous that, if we were to present them all in narrative form, the story would require a volume. More useful, however, will be a brief summary, to which we may add more ample accounts of certain notably typical cases.

The three main types of which our period offers instances are: 1.) independent rulers, recently converted and free from external pressure, exerting influence over their own country-men; 2.) monarchs of Christian lands extending their pro-tection to missionaries among weaker or dependent neigh-boring peoples; and 3.) Christian conquerors exercising force against alien non-Christian races. England and Scandinavia supply us with the best examples of the first type; the Frank-ish rulers aiding Willibrord and Boniface are of the second type; and the third can be illustrated by the campaigns of Charlemagne against the Saxons and of the Teutonic Knights in East Prussia.

The first instance in England of coöperation between king and missionary is that afforded by Ethelbert of Kent and Augustine. When Augustine and his companions arrived from Rome in 597, Ethelbert was King of Kent and *de facto* overlord of all the Anglo-Saxon states of Britain except the northern Kingdom of Northumbria (Bernicia and Deira). His wife, the daughter of the Frankish Charibert, King of Neustria, was a Christian. Ethelbert received the Roman mission with courtesy, provided its members with living quarters, and gave them freedom to preach and make con-verts. Within less than a year he himself was converted; and thanks to his generous support and the favor which he showed to all who followed his example, the people of Kent became nominally Christian within seven or eight years.

The rôle of Ethelbert in Kent was repeated with variations in all the other kingdoms of the Heptarchy, as by Sigbert in East Anglia, Peada and Oswy in Mercia, Coinwalch in Wessex, and Ethelwald in Sussex. More full of interesting detail, however, is our record of the conversion of Northumbria under Edwin and Oswald, a case of royal activity so true to type that it deserves extensive treatment, with frequent quotation from Bede's *Ecclesiastical History*.[1]

In the case of Edwin of Northumbria the resemblance to Ethelbert is especially close: he too, for a time, was the most powerful monarch in England, and he too began his relations with Christianity by marrying a Christian wife. After spending his youth in exile, Edwin, allied with Redwald of East Anglia, defeated Ethelfrid of Bernicia at the Battle of the Idle in 616 or 617 and became king of all Northumbria. He subsequently extended his power so that "he had overlordship over all the nations who inhabit Britain, both English and British, except only the people of Kent," and is therefore classed by Bede as the fifth Bretwalda. Though most of the offensive wars which won him this position took place after 625, he was already the foremost king in England when in that year he sent ambassadors to Kent to ask King Eadbald for the hand of his sister Ethelberg. Since Ethelberg was a Christian and Edwin a pagan, Eadbald insisted on making the same arrangements which Charibert had made with Ethelbert upon the latter's marriage to Bertha. The new queen and all her entourage were to be given leave "to follow their faith, and worship after the custom of the Christians." In accepting these conditions Edwin made the further promise that he himself would seriously consider embracing Christianity.

The man who was chosen to be Ethelberg's confessor, however, was destined to play a more active part than Bertha's Bishop Liudhard. Paulinus, who had been sent to England with other missionaries in 601, was selected as the queen's chaplain and ordained bishop by Archbishop Justus on July 21, 625. Soon afterward he accompanied the royal party on its journey to Northumbria; and once established at the court there, "he labored much, not only to retain those

[1] The story of the conversion of Northumbria is found in Bede's Ecclesiastical History, Book II, chs. 5, 9, 12, 13, 14, 16, 20 and Book III, chs. 1, 2, 3, 5, 6, 9, 15, 17. The notes in C. Plummer's Latin edition are particularly valuable. The quotations throughout this section are from Sellar's translation of Bede.

that went with him, by the help of God, that they should not abandon the faith, but, if haply he might, to convert some of the pagans to the grace of the faith by his preaching." But for at least a year he met with little or no success.

On the night of April 19, 626, two events occurred which deeply stirred the king. He barely escaped assassination at the hands of an emissary from King Cuichelm of Wessex, and almost at the same hour his queen gave birth to a daughter. Encouraged by Paulinus to attribute to the Christian God the safe delivery of Ethelberg and his own escape as well, Edwin permitted the bishop to baptize his daughter and promised that if he achieved victory in battle with King Cuichelm, "he would renounce his idols and serve Christ." Accordingly, on June 7, 626, the baby Eanfled and eleven others of the household were baptized. After defeating the West Saxons in the field, Edwin "took heed earnestly to be instructed at leisure by the venerable Paulinus in the knowledge of the faith, and to confer with such as he knew to be the wisest of his chief men, inquiring what they thought was fittest to be done in that case. And being a man of great natural sagacity, he often sat alone by himself a long time in silence, deliberating in the depths of his heart how he should proceed, and to what religion he should adhere."

After many months of delay Edwin reached the point of consulting his chief priest and the counsellors who constituted his Witenagemot. How accurately Bede has reported this private conference, held a century before he finished his history, we cannot be certain. But in describing the materialistic motives of the priest Coifi, the hunger for deeper religious truth expressed by one of the king's thegns, and the warming effect of Paulinus' address, the author gives the impression of recording in his own words certain genuine factors and events which served to sway the council. The upshot was a decision to renounce paganism and accept the Christian faith; and by agreement with the king the high priest Coifi himself began the new era by burning the chief temple and destroying its idols.

"King Edwin, therefore, with all the nobility of the nation, and a large number of the common sort, received the faith, and the washing of holy regeneration, in the eleventh year of his reign, which is the year of our Lord 627. . . . He was baptized at York on the holy day of Easter, being the twelfth of April" — "the birthday of the Northumbrian Church."

One of Edwin's first acts as a Christian was to grant the city of York to Paulinus as his episcopal see and to order the construction of a stone church on the site of the present cathedral. Paulinus, taking full advantage of the king's favor and coöperation, began at once the work of open evangelization, and for the next six years under Edwin's rule "preached the word of God in that country." So far as we know he was aided by only one cleric, "James the deacon, a man of zeal and great fame." It was not only with the permission of the king that Paulinus carried on his missionary labors but very often in company with the king. Still acting as court chaplain he was wont to travel with the king and queen on their tours from one royal estate to another. While the king was attending to political and financial affairs, the bishop — perhaps with his deacon — would go among the people to teach and baptize. In Deira especially "he was wont often to be with the king," but Bede cites a stay of over a month at one of the towns in Bernicia during which Paulinus was steadily occupied in preaching and baptizing. In Northumbria, therefore, Christianity was very obviously presented as the king's religion. As a result, Paulinus baptized not only two of the king's sons by his first wife and three of Ethelberg's children but also "many noble and royal persons" and large numbers of the common people. The bishop further extended his work of evangelism south of the Humber into the province of Lindsey, building a stone church at Lincoln and baptizing "a great multitude of the people in the river Trent."

This period of prosperity for the Church lasted only as long as the personal ascendancy of King Edwin and came suddenly to an end with his defeat and death. King Cadwallon, the Christian leader of the Welsh in their final struggle against the Angles, formed an alliance with the heathen King Penda of Mercia and fought against Edwin's army at the battle of Haethfelth, where "Edwin was killed on the twelfth of October in the year of our Lord 633 . . . and all his army was either slain or dispersed."

The chief results of this sudden overthrow were all disastrous for the new Church. Paulinus fled by sea to Kent with the queen and her young son and daughter, and never returned to his diocese. Osric, Edwin's cousin, became King of Deira and Eanfrid, son of the late Ethelfrid of Bernicia, fell heir to that kingdom. Osric had been baptized by Paulinus, and Eanfrid, while in exile during the reign of Edwin, had been converted in Scotland or Ireland; but both of the new monarchs at once abjured their faith. They may well have thought it easier to rally their people against the hated Christian leader Cadwallon if they marshalled them under heathen banners. In addition to suffering the loss of Christian bishop and Christian king, the country had to endure a whole year of pillage and slaughter at the hands of Penda and especially Cadwallon. By the autumn of 634 Osric had been defeated and killed and Eanfrid put to death by Cadwallon.

The wreckage of Northumbrian Christianity was as complete as the total loss of leaders and the cruel rapine of a Christian enemy could make it. But it was not as complete as certain English writers have been eager to declare. "All was lost," writes Bishop Browne, "A day's preaching [2] had converted hundreds. A day's defeat swept the whole thing away. Christianity in the North was gone."[3] "Northumbrian Christianity was a vanished dream," says Hodgkin. And Lightfoot is equally sweeping in his assertions. These sturdy British commentators are chiefly concerned to minimize the work of Paulinus, that they may magnify the en-

[2] The bishop's way of referring to six years of work by two active evangelists.
[3] Browne, *Augustine*, p. 186.

suing work of Aidan; they want to wipe the map clean of all
debt to Rome. But we cannot fairly assume so drastic a
change. It is true that wholesale conversions resulted in
wholesale apostasy. It is true also that Paulinus, as Bishop
of York, spent most of his time in Deira and had not been
able to consolidate his work in Bernicia, for, as Bede tells us,
there was at this time "no symbol of the Christian faith, no
church, no altar erected throughout all the nation of the
Bernicians." But in Deira, the chief seat of Edwin's power,
Paulinus had laid a strong and deep foundation, and he left
behind him the deacon James "who, continuing long after in
that Church, by teaching and baptizing, rescued much prey
from the ancient enemy." The successors of Paulinus had
much pioneering to do, but they did not begin at the beginning. The work of six years was not wiped out in one.

The second and more brilliant chapter in the missionary
history of Northumbria began with the victory of Oswald —
the brother of Eanfrid — who met Cadwallon and his army
in battle at Hefenfelth toward the close of 634. Cadwallon
was defeated and slain, and Oswald became undisputed
monarch of all Northumbria. According to Bede, who rates
him as the sixth Bretwalda, "he brought under his dominion
all the nations and provinces of Britain," and thereby obtained "a greater earthly kingdom than any of his ancestors."
Though this is a plain exaggeration in view of Oswald's
failure to subdue King Penda, it is undoubtedly true that he
was the strongest sovereign in England. More than that, he
was a genuine Christian of the highest character, who devoted
himself, during the eight years of his reign, to promoting the
faith in his dominions. Having been trained and baptized
among the Irish in his youth and having no connections with
the Roman mission, he naturally turned to Iona to find missionaries who might restore and nourish the wasted Church
of Northumbria. The first leader sent him by the island
monastery was a complete failure who shortly returned to
report that the English were too stubborn to be taught. The
second choice of the monks at Iona was Aidan — the most

saintly of the evangelists of Saxon England. Ordained a bishop at Iona, he reached Northumbria in the spring or early summer of 635.

"On the arrival of the bishop, the king appointed him his episcopal see in the island of Lindisfarne,[4] as he desired," — a new home with something of the solitude and beauty of his beloved Iona. "The king also humbly and willingly in all things giving ear to his admonitions, industriously applied himself to build up and extend the Church of Christ in his kingdom; wherein, when the bishop, who was not perfectly skilled in the English tongue, preached the Gospel, it was a fair sight to see the king himself interpreting the Word of God to his ealdormen and thegns, for he had thoroughly learned the language of the Scots [Irish] during his long banishment." The work of Aidan was furthered not only by the strong support of the king who "gave lands and other property . . . to found monasteries," but also by a steady stream of missionaries from Iona. As a result, "churches were built in divers places" and "the people joyfully flocked together to hear the Word." There can be found in missionary history no example more nearly perfect of a king's influence in the conversion of a people, for Oswald, throughout his reign, was not simply an important convert but an active missionary.

But once more that persistent pagan King Penda of Mercia was ready to deal a blow at his Christian neighbors. On August 5, 642 the Mercian and Northumbrian armies met at Maserfelth,[5] and King Oswald was killed "in the thirty-eighth year of his age." At his death the kingdom was divided between his brother Oswy who ruled in Bernicia and his cousin Oswin who governed in Deira. Since both were zealous Christians, no reversion to heathenism took place. Oswin especially was "a man of wonderful piety and devotion" and a close friend and supporter of Aidan. Oswy had begun his career as king by marrying Eanfled — Edwin's daughter —

[4] Near Barnborough, the capital of Bernicia.
[5] Probably at Oswestry near Shrewsbury in Shropshire.

who had been living in exile in Kent. He thus united the royal houses of Deira and Bernicia. Some eight or nine years later, for reasons that we do not know, he fell out with his cousin Oswin. Oswin declined to give battle and was murdered by Oswy's reeve on August 20, 651. Eleven days later Aidan died. He was succeeded as bishop by Finan, another monk from Iona, who governed the diocese until his death in 661. King Oswy, however, was destined to reign for another twenty years and to play a part in the conversion of Mercia and Essex.

The other great area where Christian kings were conspicuous in promoting the conversion of their own subjects is Scandinavia.

Though Anskar is commonly regarded as the Apostle to Scandinavia, the result of his devoted labors was small — "two churches on the borders of Denmark and one priest working in a Swedish commercial port."[6] Indeed, "though a certain number of adherents had been gained among the nobles and trading classes, the mass of the people remained untouched."[7] Even these small gains did not long survive him, for in both Denmark and Sweden his successors were unable to maintain their position. In fact, it was a century and a half after his death in 865 that Denmark was really converted and another one hundred and twenty years before Sweden was Christianized. The chief reason, perhaps, for the failure of this isolated effort was the violence of the Viking Age with its unbridled piracy and its constant wars. But another cause was undoubtedly the fact that Anskar depended for his royal support far less upon Danish and Swedish kings than upon the emperors Louis the Pious and Louis the German. In other words, this first introduction of Christianity was too closely bound up with the political and diplomatic relations of Northern Europe. Sharing their vicissitudes, the mission led a feeble life, and finally succumbed.

In Denmark it was not until Harald Bluetooth entered in 935 on his reign of fifty years that the feeble Christian com-

---

[6] Hauck, vol. II, p. 684.   [7] Camb. Med. Hist., vol. III, pp. 314 ff.

munity could count upon royal support. Beginning as a benevolent neutral, Harald was converted within ten years and thenceforth became a positive factor in the advance of Christianity, founding churches and calling missionaries to active service in his realm. After his death, however, there followed an interval of some fifteen years when the Church suffered persecution and paganism revived. But in the year 1000 the tide turned with the accession of Svein, who had already accepted baptism in England and who steadfastly exerted his royal authority in aid of the Church. His successor, Knut the Great, was a no less active supporter of the new and struggling Christian community in Denmark. To the zeal of a devout Christian he added the wisdom of a statesman who saw in the Church an instrument for civilizing the people and a strong ally of the state. The thorough and final establishment of Christianity in Denmark was the work of his reign.

In spite of feeble missionary efforts from German headquarters at Bremen, the Church in Sweden remained negligible until the end of the eleventh century. Its growth thereafter was due less to organized missions than to the effect of commercial and political intercourse with Christian lands, especially with England. One result was the conversion of the first Swedish king to embrace Christianity, Olof Skötkonung, who was baptized by Bishop Sigurd in 1008. Under his successor Anund Jacob (1024–1051) Christianity enjoyed the continuance of royal favor and grew ever more widely diffused. Thereafter the intervals of pagan reaction were few and relatively brief, the fortunes of the new religion reflecting in every case the attitude and temper of the ruler. The period of conversion ended with the long reign of Sverker (1130–1205), who was a devout and active Christian deeply concerned to establish the young Swedish Church on a firm basis and to extend its influence. It was he who laid the foundations of the cathedral at Uppsala, that old stronghold of heathenism, working into it the materials of the ancient pagan temple. At his invitation, too, monks of the Cistercian

Order established the first monasteries in the land. And finally, three years before his death, the visit of the papal legate Nicholas Brakespeare brought the Church of Sweden into definite relations with the papacy.

The conversion of Norway to Christianity was mainly due to the energetic initiative and the systematic methods of two Christian kings — Olaf Tryggvason (995–1000) and Olaf Haraldson (1015–1030). But their speedy success in establishing Christianity as the religion of their people was made possible by the changes wrought in Norway during the preceding two centuries of the Viking Age.[8]

The raids of the Norse vikings upon the coasts of England and the continent, beginning in the latter part of the eighth century, and the voyages of peaceful traders to the same lands brought to Norway the first signs of Christian influence. These varied types of voyagers were continually returning home, often bringing with them Christian captives, so that the knowledge of Christianity spread to some extent throughout the general population. Especially among nobles and warriors the effect was to break down faith in the ancient gods and to qualify the old unquestioning loyalty to traditional paganism.

If this undermining of the old faith was one prerequisite to the work of the two Olafs, the unification of the country was another. That had been achieved by Harald Fairhair, the founder of the Kingdom of Norway, who reigned as overlord from 872 to 930. During this long period the country retained its unity but remained entirely pagan. Between 934 and 970, however, there were two Christian kings in Norway, Hákon the Good and Harald Greyskin, but neither was able to make headway against the strength of paganism.

It was Olaf Tryggvason who was the real founder of the Church in Norway, for he was the first monarch to share the

---

[8] The term *viking* is a derivative of the Old Norse *vik*, a creek, bay, or fjord, and means one who haunts such an opening and uses it as a base whence raids may be made on the surrounding country. The word is now commonly applied to those Norsemen, Danes, and Swedes who harried the British Isles and the coasts of Europe from the eighth to the eleventh centuries. Camb. Med. Hist., vol. III, p. 309.

indomitable zeal of a real missionary. Like other Christianizing kings, his motives were no doubt mixed. He would naturally profit by the example of rulers in Christian lands and note the status accorded to them by their subjects and by their fellow-rulers. Nor would he fail to realize that his own kingdom, so insecurely unified, could not depend for support on the ancient social and religious system, whereas the Christian Church, once firmly founded, would bring stability to the kingdom and win for its king new dignity both at home and abroad. Yet these motives and purposes were only auxiliary to the force of a genuine crusading ardor. His career as missionary king is recounted with such racy vigor in the fascinating pages of the Heimskringla that we are justified in giving some attention to its details.

The great-grandson of Harald Fairhair, Olaf, was born about 964. Much of his youth he spent in various viking cruises, raiding the coasts of Scotland, Ireland, and England. On one of these voyages we are told that he was baptized by a hermit in the Scilly Isles, and on the reliable authority of the Anglo-Saxon Chronicle we learn that he was confirmed by a bishop in England in the year 994. The following summer Olaf determined that the time was ripe to win for himself the kingdom of his great-grandfather (then in the hands of the pagan Hákon Jarl) and set sail with a fleet for Norway. By that time the people had turned against Hákon, so that Olaf met with an unexpectedly warm reception. Hákon was soon murdered by one of his own servants and Olaf was welcomed as a deliverer and accepted as king by a general *thing* or public assembly at Trondhjem.

Olaf was now ready to begin his missionary career. Aided by the previous work of kings and missionaries, whose pioneer efforts we have described, and profiting by the popular reaction against the murdered pagan Hákon Jarl, he found his task less formidable than might have been expected. From the beginning his Christian convictions were no secret and had proved no obstacle. He brought with him from England not only a number of priests but also Bishop Sigurd, who probably came from one of the Norse settlements in North-umbria and who remained his friend and counsellor during the five years of his eventful and vigorous reign. The missionary campaign was wisely begun in Viken where the king's relatives were powerful and where Christian influence had long been familiar.

"When Olaf Tryggvason became King of Norway he stayed a long time during the summer in Viken. There came to him many of his kinsmen, some that were allied to him and many who had been his father's good friends. He welcomed them with great love. Olaf then called to him his mother's brothers, his stepfather Lodin and his brothers-in-law Torgeir and Hyrning. And with the greatest warmth he put before them a matter which they should take up with him and afterwards help on with all their skill, namely, that he intended to have Christianity throughout the whole of his kingdom. He said he would set out to convert all Norway to Christianity or otherwise die. . . . All these men agreed to do as he bade and, together with those who would follow their advice, to help him in everything he wished. King Olaf straight-way opened the matter with the common folk, that he would ask all men in his kingdom to become Christian. Those who had already promised to do so agreed first to that behest, and they were the mightiest present: all the others followed them. Thereupon all the men in the east of Viken were baptized. Now the king went north in Viken and bade all men take up Christianity, and those who spoke against it he dealt with hard; some he slew, some he maimed, and some he drove away from the land. . . . And in that summer and the following winter the folk in the whole of Viken were all converted to Christianity."[9] We thus find that even in his earliest efforts, where opposition was least determined, Olaf was ready to use ruthless force.

After completing the religious conquest of Viken, the king turned his attention to Agder, the southernmost part of Norway. "And at every place where he held a *thing* with the

[9] Heimskringla, Saga of Olaf Tryggvason, c. 53. Monsen's translation.

bonders [free land-holders] he bade men be baptized, and all men took up Christianity, for none of the bonders dared oppose the king, and wherever he went the folk were baptized." [10] This procedure was typical of his subsequent missionary activity: the forms of racial democracy were observed, but force, when not exercised, appeared menacingly in reserve. After similar success in Rogaland, north of Agder, "King Olaf proceeded with his folk to the Gula *Thing* [held on the coast at the Sogne Fjord in the northern part of Hordaland], for the bonders had sent word that there they would answer this matter of his. . . . When [the chiefs] were all gathered he put forth his errand and bade them be baptized according to his behest. Then said Almod the Old: 'We kinsmen have spoken about this matter among ourselves and we all shall be of one counsel. If thou, O King, thinkest to drive us kinsmen to such things, to break our laws and break us under thee by force, then shall we withstand thee with all our might and may fate then decide the victory. But if thou, O King, wilt give us kinsmen some useful gifts, then wilt thou do a right thing and we shall all turn to thee in full obedience.' The king said: 'What will ye crave of me, that our peace be of the best?'. Then said Almod: 'First, that thou wilt wed thy sister Astrid to our kinsman Erling Skjalgson . . .' The king said that it seemed likely that it would be a good wedding, as Erling was of good lineage and of goodly looks, but still, he said, Astrid herself must answer that matter . . . and the end of it was that Astrid was betrothed to Erling. Then the king called the *thing* and bade the bonders take up Christianity. Almod and Erling were the foremost men in promoting this matter of the king and with them were all their kinsmen. No one had spoken against it and so all the folk were baptized and converted to Christianity." [11]

Working systematically northward, Olaf next summoned a *thing* to meet at Dragseid in the Stadt peninsula, where representatives of four of the neighboring districts gathered, and

[10] Heimskringla, Saga of Olaf Tryggvason, c. 54. Monsen's translation.
[11] *Ibid.*, cc. 56, 57.

where likewise, under threat of force, the bonders submitted to baptism. All of southern and western Norway had now surrendered to the threatening invitations of their Christian king and he had reached at last the strongly pagan area that centered around the Trondhjem Fjord where he was to encounter the first vigorous opposition.

Entering the fjord, he landed at Hlade, burned the famous temple there and carried off all its sacred ornaments; but when the indignant people rose in arms, he yielded for the time being and sailed northward along the coast to Hálogaland. Finding the same hostility there, he changed his plans and slowly sailed southward back to Viken. In the following summer Olaf reappeared at Trondhjem with an army and called a meeting of the Frosta *Thing* which represented eight districts of that region. "And when the king came to the *thing* the body of bonders were come there fully weaponed. When the *thing* met, the king spoke to the folk and bade them take up Christianity. And when he had spoken for a little time the bonders shouted and bade him be quiet, saying that otherwise they would go against him and drive him away. . . . And when King Olaf saw the heated temper of the bonders and likewise that they had so great an army that he could not withstand them, he changed his speech" and agreed to meet with them again for the midsummer offering at the great pagan center nearby at Maeren. "Then," he said, "we shall take counsel about what worship we shall have and we shall all be as one about it."[12]

Some time before the meeting at Maeren Olaf held a great feast at Hlade for the leading chiefs of the neighborhood, and after the guests had spent the night in drunken slumber he surrounded them with armed men from his ships and gave them the choice of accepting Christianity or becoming sacrificial victims at the coming celebration at Maeren. In the face of overwhelming force they submitted, agreed to baptism, and gave hostages to the king. Having thus disposed of part of his opponents, he was ready to appear at

[12] *Ibid.*, c. 65.

Maeren with his forces. "The king had the *thing* called and both troops went to it fully weaponed. And when the *thing* was met, the king spoke and bade the men become Christian." The ringleader of the pagans, Iron-Skeggi, replied, "'We wish thee, O King, to sacrifice as other kings have done here before thee.' To this speech the bonders gave a great applause. . . . The king said he would go into the temple and see their worship when they sacrificed. That pleased the bonders well, and so both troops went to the temple."[13] But Olaf had no intention of submitting. Entering the temple with a few of his men, he struck down the image of Thor with his axe, while his followers overthrew the other idols. "And whilst the king was in the temple Iron-Skeggi was slain outside the temple door; the king's men did it. When the king came out to his men he bade the bonders choose between two things: one was that they should all take up Christianity, and the other was that they should hold battle with him. But after the fall of Skeggi there was no leader in the bonders' army to raise the standard against King Olaf, so what they chose was to go to the king and do as he bade. King Olaf had all the folk who were there baptized and took hostages of the bonders that they should hold to Christianity. After that King Olaf let his men go round all the folk districts in Trondhjem; no man spoke against Christianity and all the folk in Trondlaw were baptized."[14]

There remained now only one region of importance which had not yet submitted to Christianity — the northern area of Hálogaland. So "the next spring Olaf had his ships and men fitted out. The king himself had the *Crane* and a great and very fine army. And when he was ready he sailed with it out of the fjord, then north by Byrda and so north into Hálogaland. And wherever he came to land he held *things* and bade all the folk there take baptism and the true faith. No one had the strength to speak against him and all the land became Christian wherever he went. . . . The king then sailed north

[13] Heimskringla, Saga of Olaf Tryggvason, c. 68. Monsen's translation.
[14] *Ibid.*, c. 69.

as far as Amd, and there all the folk took up Christianity."[15]
The few remaining chiefs who maintained the cause of paganism were either won over or slain. But Raud the strong, who was powerful in one of the northern fjords, remained bitterly irreconcilable. Olaf, however, finally succeeded in capturing him while he was asleep in his house, and since he would not submit, had him tortured to death. "He made all the men who had followed Raud be baptized, but those who would not he caused to be slain or tormented." Olaf then "christened the whole fjord and afterwards went his way to the south along the land."[16]

Within four years King Olaf had brought about the formal Christianization of Norway and from that time on no general heathen reaction of importance disturbed the slow progress of the Church. But Olaf's reign was drawing to a close. In the summer of the year 1000, returning from an expedition to Vendland to recover some of the estates of his wife, he was attacked by the fleet of the Danish King Svein near Rügen. Defeated by tremendous odds, Olaf was badly wounded, disappeared from sight in the mêlée, and was undoubtedly drowned.

Sixteen years later, after a period of disunion during which Christianity diminished in influence, Olaf Haraldson, who had been baptized in Rouen, seized the throne of Norway and began the chief work of his reign — the reunification and the further Christianization of his kingdom. In view of the previous activity of Tryggvason his task was rather to organize and consolidate than to pioneer. The mass baptisms of twenty years earlier and the destruction of idols and temples may have had little effect on the lives of a people still pagan in substance, but they had lowered the prestige of the ancient religion and loosened the bonds which attached men to their gods. The very fact that the folk of Norway were nominally Christian and, in form at least, had accepted the new faith gave their king a right to undertake that process of organization and enforcement which was his main achieve-

[15] *Ibid.*, cc. 77, 79.   [16] *Ibid.*, cc. 78–80.

ment. The further facts that there was no regular pagan priesthood and that no deliberate reaction had since taken place made progress the less difficult. As in Tryggvason's time, political motives and ends were mingled with religious, for the development of the Church and the consolidation of the kingdom under one rule were part of the same process, so that "it is hard to say whether the king's journeys through Norway more nearly resembled an episcopal visitation or a royal progress."[17]

The organization of local churches and the remolding of law in the light of the Christian morality of that day were definite ends which he began at once to pursue. In this work he was everywhere aided, as our sources assure us, by bishops and priests of the Anglo-Saxon Church whom he had brought with him to Norway. His customary mode of procedure was to visit one district after another, accompanied by several hundred armed retainers and a group of clergy. He would inspect religious and moral conditions, summon a *thing*, secure agreement upon certain Christian laws, and before leaving would appoint a priest to care for the local community and perhaps consecrate a church. By 1021, after Olaf had ruled Norway for nearly seven years, there were but few regions left which had not felt the energy of his reforming zeal; and within the next two or three years these backward areas were vigorously visited and submitted to royal force. The fact that all Norway had by then become nominally Christian was almost wholly due to the indomitable persistence of the king guided and aided by his English clergy.

"The first ten years of [Olaf's] rule were to his use and honor, but afterwards all his plans were heavy and difficult, and everything he tried his luck at always went against him."[18] King Knut, who was then ruling over England, Scotland, Wales, and Denmark, claimed also the throne of Norway. And it was to Knut that many of Olaf's nobles, restive under his firm and strenuous rule, began now to turn. Defections became numerous after 1025 and moved Olaf in

17 Willson, p. 69.   18 Heimskringla, Saga of St. Olaf, c. 187.

1027 to join forces with the King of Sweden and attack Knut in an indecisive naval battle off the coast of Sweden. Within the next two years, however, Knut had subjugated Norway and driven Olaf into exile in Russia. Thence he was persuaded to return, only to meet his death at the great battle of Stiklestad on July 29, 1030.

Almost at once, however, popular feeling in Norway underwent a strong revulsion. "This winter," says Snorri, "talk arose amongst men in Trondhjem that King Olaf was a holy man, and that many tokens witnessing his holiness occurred. Many began praying to King Olaf about matters which seemed weightiest to them. Many got help from these prayers, some got their health, and some had good luck on their journeys or in other matters as they thought needful."[19] Thus simply the saga describes the canonization of Olaf, for as Saint Olaf he was thenceforth the center of the most popular cult in Norway.

We have so far considered the missionary activity of independent rulers, recently Christianized, who exerted a voluntary influence over their own countrymen. But, as we have seen, there was another type of royal auxiliary — monarchs of Christian lands who extended their protection to missionaries among weaker or dependent peoples. And of this variety the Frankish rulers who aided Willibrord and Boniface are excellent examples.

Few medieval missionaries were more obviously dependent upon favorable political conditions for the success of their work than was Willibrord. In general terms, his success was in proportion to the extent to which his field of labor was under Frankish control. He prospered where and when the "mayors of the palace" could give him protection and support.

In the seventh century Frisia was an ill-defined territory with shifting boundaries. It extended roughly from the mouth of the Ems in the north to the mouth of the Scheldt in

[19] *Ibid.*, c. 241.

the south, with a variable depth from the coast inland. The southern part had been brought under control by Dagobert I (King of the Franks, 629–639) who made Utrecht a Frankish city; but after his death the Frisians retook the abandoned area, and when Willibrord arrived in Frisia in 690 Utrecht was in possession of its native King Radbod.

The pagan Radbod was the first foreign ruler with whom Willibrord came into contact, and the prospects in his domain were so unfavorable that the missionary immediately sought the protection of Pippin, the Frankish major domus. As Alcuin relates, "Pippin [20] received him with all honor; but as he was unwilling to deprive himself and his people of so great a teacher, he assigned to him suitable localities within the bounds of his own realm where he could uproot the thorns of idolatry and scatter more abundantly the pure seed of God's Word." [21] Or, as Bede records it, Willibrord and his companions "turned aside to Pippin, duke of the Franks, and were friendly entertained of him; and because he had lately taken hither Frisland [i.e., the southwest parts of Frisia nearest to the Franks] and driven out thence their king Rathbod, he sent them thither to preach; aiding them also with his own princely authority, that no man should bring any hindrance to their preaching, and bountifully rewarding such as should be ready to receive the faith; whereby it came to pass by the assistance of God's grace, that in short time they converted many from idolatry to the faith of Christ." [22]

It is thus plain from our sources that, because of the need for political protection, Willibrord began his enterprise in a half-Christian territory, partly Frankish in population but mainly Frisian. It was Pippin, moreover, who was so encouraged by the first success of the new missionary that he took the initiative in sending him to Rome for consecration

[20] Pippin of Heristal, the Austrasian Mayor of the Palace and real ruler of the Franks, who, after the battle of Testry (687), had established the control of his family over both Austrasia and Neustria.

[21] Alcuin, *Vita Willibrordi*, c. 5. Grieve's translation.

[22] Bede, H. E., V, 10. King's translation.

as bishop. It was undoubtedly at this time, too, that Pippin assigned to him as his see the city of Utrecht which then seems to have been in Frankish hands. Within five years, after the further extension of Frankish control in Frisia and a new peace with King Radbod, Pippin established Willibrord as archbishop of a new province which included the whole of Frisia. The aims and influence of the major domus, then, are clearly evident both in the assignment of the bishop to his sphere of labor and in the organization of that growing area. From this time forward the ties of Willibrord and his mission with the Frankish state, no less than with Rome, were firmly bound.

The successful Frankish aggression which had evidently resulted, before Willibrord's consecration, in the possession of Utrecht and in a new agreement with Radbod, marked the beginning of a brief era of peaceful relations between the two rulers and their peoples, signalized in 711 by the marriage of Radbod's daughter Theutsind to Pippin's son Grimoald. During this period, therefore, Willibrord was able to take full advantage of the comparatively favorable attitude of the king who was ready at last to welcome him and to permit the return of others who had been driven out because of their connection with the Franks.

It is in this period that we may place the narrative of Alcuin which tells us that "this man of God . . . sought to direct the streams of heavenly teaching beyond the confines of the Frankish kingdom. He did not fear to wait upon Radbod, then King of the Frisians, and, like his subjects, a pagan; and wherever he went he proclaimed God's Word with full confidence. But while the Frisian king received the man of God kindly and in humility, no application of the Word of Life could soften that heart of stone, and when the man of God saw that he could win no fruit there, he turned his missionary course to the savage tribes of the Danes." [23] Here we may note not only the dependence of Willibrord upon Radbod for his freedom to preach but also his failure

[23] Alcuin, c. 9.

to make progress as long as the king remained obdurate. As a result of these attempts to advance in purely pagan Frisia, Willibrord returned to work in the more congenial area of Frankish Frisia where paganism was not undiluted and where he could remain under the immediate patronage of Pippin. And there his efforts prospered.

But another shift in the political scene was at hand, imperilling the missionary cause. In 714 Pippin died, and there ensued a civil war between powerful factions disputing the succession. Radbod, allying himself with one party, took advantage of the situation to persecute the Christian clergy, destroy most of their churches, and reëstablish the heathen sanctuaries. By the year 718, however, Charles Martel, after a series of victories, won control of the greater part of his father's dominions and conquered Radbod. Finally, in 719, Radbod died and was succeeded by his son Aldgisl II who was a professed Christian.

From 719 onward, with a Christian king in Frisia and with Charles Martel, the champion of the Christian Church, established as the ruler of Neustria and Austrasia, all the political forces were at last favorable to the missionary work of Willibrord. He resumed his see at Utrecht, welcomed Boniface as his assistant (719–721), and "having thus obtained a larger opportunity for evangelization, he sought by means of sacred baptism to purify the people recently won by the sword." [24] And for the remaining twenty years of his life his work prospered as never before.

Boniface, the greatest of all medieval missionaries, began his career upon the continent by an abortive attempt to enter Frisia in 716. Having learned, during this first venture, the value of royal support and the fatal results of royal opposition, he was the more eager that his future work should be fortified, wherever possible, by the patronage of rulers. His two years of subsequent labor with Willibrord (719–721) mark the end of Boniface's work as a subordinate and the beginning of his career as an apostle in those regions of Ger-

[24] Alcuin, c. 13.

many to which he had been assigned by the Pope. After his initial successes in Hesse during the years 721 and 722, he sent a report of his work to Gregory II who invited him to Rome and consecrated him bishop on November 30, 722. In December the Pope gave him a letter to Charles Martel, major domus of the Frankish kingdom.

This letter is mentioned by Willibald in his Life of Boniface, and its results are described in these words: "After Boniface by long and devious ways had visited the territories of great peoples, he came to the aforesaid prince of the Franks, and was received by him with veneration. He delivered to Duke Charles the letter of the above-mentioned Roman bishop and of the apostolic see, and, subject to his lordship and patronage, returned, with the consent of Duke Charles, to the land of the Hessians where before he had tarried." [25]

The patronage and the consent of which Willibald speaks were expressed in a letter of Charles Martel written in the spring of 723. [26]

"To the holy lords and apostolic Fathers in Christ, the bishops; to the dukes, counts, deputies (*vicarii*), stewards, agents, officers, messengers, and friends; the illustrious Charles, major domus, your well-wisher.

"Know that the apostolic Father in Christ, Boniface the bishop, has come to us, and has begged that we should take him under our protection and defence. Know that we have with glad mind done this. Therefore we have thus ordered it and we have had prepared for him this document ratified by our own hand. Wheresoever he goes he must be preserved quiet and safe in our love, protection, and defence; on this condition, that he does justice, and receives justice likewise. And if any difficulty arise which cannot be decided by the law, he must be left quiet and safe to our judgment, both he and his, so that no one shall do anything troublesome or harmful to him. And that the surer credence may be given

[25] Willibald, c. 6. Robinson's translation.
[26] Ep. 22. Browne's translation, pp. 61 f., revised by Tangl's text and translation.

to this, I have confirmed it at the foot with my own hand and we have sealed it with our ring."

There are several reasons why Charles should have been ready to assume so promptly the protection of Boniface. In the first place, it is not unlikely that he had met and consulted with the missionary on a previous occasion. But more important is the fact that the receipt of this letter from the Pope was a great event in the life of Charles. The Pope, probably writing to him for the first time, recognizes him as the leading man in France. To one who had been struggling hard against opponents for a long time and at last held the kingdom united under his leadership this papal recognition was a cherished prize, and to grant a favor to the man who bore it was not difficult. In other words, it was not enthusiasm for church expansion or for Boniface as a foreign missionary that moved Charles, but a readiness to exert an authority practically royal and to live up to the dominant part assigned to him by the Pope. In the letter of commendation, however, he never mentions the papacy, and though he recognizes Boniface as bishop in the mission field assigned by the Pope, he clearly states that Boniface, in turn, is to recognize his overlordship.

The protection offered by Charles was of high value to Boniface and unquestionably gave him a standing in Hesse and Thuringia which he would otherwise have lacked. The attitude of the numerous Frankish officials in his field must have been markedly influenced by their knowledge of the patronage which Charles had extended. But so far as direct material support of his missionary work was concerned, Charles and his subordinates supplied no further help. The close and friendly relations which existed between Charles and Willibrord in Frisia did not obtain in the case of Boniface, nor could the latter count upon the generous financial aid which the Frankish ruler lavished upon the church at Utrecht.

The only remaining evidence of any missionary assistance from Charles is contained in a letter from Gregory III to Boniface, dated October 29, 739, in which the Pope says,

"You have told us of the heathen people of Germany whom our God of his pity has freed from the power of the pagans and to the number of a hundred thousand souls has gathered into the bosom of holy mother Church by means of your efforts and the help of Charles, prince of the Franks." [27]

At his death in October 741 Charles Martel left three sons — Pippin and Karlmann by his marriage with Chrotrud, and Gripho by his marriage with Swanahild. Boniface had no knowledge of what arrangements might have been made for the succession or of how the kingdom was to be divided, and he was naturally anxious to keep as clear as possible from the political difficulties likely to arise. He therefore wrote almost identical letters to all three brothers asking for their aid and protection in his work. The surviving letter to Gripho indicates Boniface's sense of dependence on the Frankish rulers and the kind of help he expected from them.

"I beseech and adjure your piety," writes Boniface, "that, if God shall have given you the power, you study to aid the servants of God, the bishops and presbyters who are in Thuringia, and to defend the monks and handmaids of Christ against the malice of pagans, and to help the Christian people that the pagans destroy them not. . . ." [28]

As it turned out, however, Karlmann assumed control of Austrasia, Thuringia, and Swabia, and Pippin of Neustria and Burgundy, while Gripho came to figure only as a rebellious trouble-maker. It was with Karlmann and Pippin, then, that Boniface maintained friendly relations and with whom he coöperated in his expanding labors; and it is of their assistance that he writes to Bishop Daniel of Winchester some time between 742 and 746: "Without the protection of the King of the Franks I can neither rule the people of the Church nor defend the priests and clergy, the monks and nuns of God; nor can I avail to check even the heathen rites and the worship of idols in Germany without his mandate, and the fear of him." [29]

[27] Ep. 45. Browne's translation, p. 95.
[28] Ep. 48. Browne's translation, pp. 363 f.   [29] Ep. 63. Kylie's translation.

The coöperation between Boniface and the sons of Charles Martel was concerned, for the most part, with the reformation of the Frankish Church — the calling of synods, the enforcement of discipline among the clergy, etc., all of which is aside from our proper subject of Boniface's mission to the heathen. But that their protecting care extended also to his evangelistic enterprises is made plain by the letter he wrote to Abbot Fulrad of St. Denis in 752, two years before his death. About to depart for Frisia where he was soon to suffer martyrdom, Boniface felt deeply concerned for the future welfare of the many English men and women who had come out to work with him in Hesse and Thuringia and who looked to him for every kind of support. Writing to Fulrad but evidently intending the letter to be read by Pippin, Boniface begs "that in my name you will salute our glorious and lovable king, Pippin, and give him great thanks for all the works of piety he has done for me, and will lay before him what I and my friends think likely to happen. It seems to us that by reason of these infirmities of mine I must soon end this temporal life and the course of my days. Wherefore I pray our king's highness . . . that he would deign to inform and command me, while I still live, about my disciples, what means of support he will after my death provide for them. For almost all of them are foreigners. Some are priests, appointed in many places to minister to church and people; some are monks in our cells, and young boys set to learn to read; and some are old and have for a long time lived with me and labored and helped me. I am anxious about all of these, that they may not be dispersed after my death, but may receive from your highness the means of subsistence and protection and be not scattered as sheep not having a shepherd; and that the people near the borders of the pagans may not lose the law of Christ. . . . But this especially I beg may be assured, because my priests near the pagan march lead a miserable life. Bread to eat they can obtain, but clothing they cannot find there unless they obtain from elsewhere counsel and support, in order to be able to live and endure in those places for the ministry of the people, in the same way that I have helped them." [30]

As Bishop Browne says, "It seems reasonable to gather from this most touching letter that Boniface had received his principal supplies for the maintenance of such of the work of his mission as was conducted in newly established churches and monasteries from the dukes of the Franks. . . ." [31]

That Pippin granted these requests we learn from a letter of Boniface addressed to the king in the following year in which he says, "We give great thanks to the clemency of your highness, and we pray our Lord Jesus Christ that he will give you eternal reward in the kingdom of the heavens, because you have deigned kindly to hear our petitions and have comforted my old age and infirmity." [32]

Finally, in May 753, Boniface went to Pippin's court in Neustria and secured his protection for the Frisian bishopric and his consent to the missionary expedition which was about to be launched, and which ended in his death.

Our historical examples of the relation between kings and missionaries have so far been of two varieties — first, rulers more or less peacefully helping to convert their own subjects, and second, monarchs protecting and advancing the work of missionaries among neighboring peoples. A third type remains to be considered — that of Christian political leaders who united the aims of conquest and Christianization by the use of the sword against alien non-Christian races. In these cases royal aid, from the Christian point of view, was least valuable and least admirable, since the form it took was that of imperial expansion and compulsory colonization. The military and political elements in the process usually neutralized and often obliterated the religious; and the missionaries, instead of being honored pioneers who took the initiative, became merely royal servants or pawns in the imperial game. The story of such instances is therefore of

[30] Ep. 93. Browne's translation, pp. 265 f., with corrections.
[31] Browne, p. 266.   [32] Ep. 107. Browne's translation, p. 267.

relatively small interest and may well be summarized with brevity.

The outstanding examples are the conquest of the Saxons by Charlemagne, the conquest of the Wends in the succeeding centuries, and the conquest of the East Prussians which did not end until near the close of the thirteenth century. Since the subject of Prussia, involving as it does the power of the papacy, will be treated in a later chapter, we shall deal here only with the tragic story of the Saxons and the Wends.

"With Charles ambition and religion worked together. Successes in arms were for him at the same time successes for Christianity. The ecclesiastical motive was specially strong in the Saxon wars. And the Saxons resisted ecclesiastical subjection as much as political. They struggled with their utmost strength against the Franks for their political freedom and for the imaginary blessings of their national religion." [33]

The Saxon people were divided into three main tribes — the Westphalians in the valley of the Ems, the Engers in the valley of the Weser, and Eastphalians between the Engers and the river Elbe. At the beginning of Charlemagne's reign they still lived in small independent political communities under local chieftains, combining temporarily only in time of war. They were characterized by an ardent devotion to their native religion. There is no sure evidence of the existence of any Christian churches in Saxon territory before the reign of Charlemagne, and it was under his leadership that the Frankish power first exerted deliberate pressure toward the north.

The first campaign was decided upon at the Imperial Assembly at Worms in the summer of 772. Invading the territory of the Engers, Charlemagne captured their fortified camp of Eresburg (Obermarsberg) on the Diemel and burned the sacred grove which surrounded it, destroying the famous wooden column called the Irminsul which was honored as

[33] Camb. Med. Hist., vol. II, pp. 609 f. The chief sources for the Saxon campaigns are the Annals listed in the Bibliography — the *Annales Laurissenses, Einhardi, Mettenses,* and *Fuldenses.*

the symbolic bearer of the universe. He then marched eastward to the Weser where the Engers offered their submission
and gave twelve hostages. The fact that this was primarily a
punitive expedition and that nothing was said of religion in
the peace terms indicates that the conversion of the Saxons
was not then the king's main object. But the destruction of
the Irminsul had roused religious motives to unite with
political.

How this expedition and others to follow were interpreted
by a contemporary of Charlemagne we learn from an interesting passage in Eigil's Life of Sturmi, the famous Abbot of
Fulda. "When the lord King Charles had reigned happily for
four years [772] the Saxon people were still savage and most
hostile in every way and wholly given over to heathen practices. But King Charles, always devoted to the Lord (for he
was a most Christian man), began to consider how he might
win this people to Christ. After he had listened to the counsel of the servants of God, he asked them to prevail upon the
Lord through their prayers that He might look with favor
upon his desires. Then, after he had brought together a great
army and had invoked the name of Christ, he set out for
Saxony. He took with him a throng of clergy-abbots and
priests — all orthodox defenders of the faith, that they might
cause the people (who from the beginning of the world had
lain bound in the chains of the Evil Spirit) to take upon
them, as believers, the mild and gentle yoke of Christ.
When the king came thither he converted the greater part of
that people to the faith of Christ, partly by the sword, partly
by persuasion, and partly through gifts. Not long after he
divided every province into episcopal districts and gave to
the servants of the Lord power to teach and to baptize. At
that time the care of the greater part of the people was entrusted to the blessed Sturmi who, since the office of preaching was assigned to him, made it his business in every way to
win no small number of the people to the Lord. He utilized
his favorable opportunity and taught them through holy
sermons to abandon their idols and shrines, to receive the

faith of Christ, to destroy the temples of their gods, to cut down their sacred groves, and to build sacred churches." [34]

Throughout this brief account we are reminded of the crusading element in these expeditions of Charlemagne, in response to which the whole enterprise was readily interpreted as a fight against the powers of Satan; and we note the mingling of methods forceful and persuasive — the well-trained army and the corps of clergy as parts of one united program.

The history of the next twenty years is simply a story of successive rebellions put down with vindictive energy and followed by extending conquests. Each time the religious element bulked larger than before and each time large crowds accepted baptism. But a stubborn minority under the Saxon chief Widukind was hard to subdue. Even the cold-blooded murder of forty-five hundred captives in 782 led only to further fighting. But three years later Widukind himself surrendered and submitted to baptism, a notable victory for "Christianity" which the Pope celebrated by appointing three days of festival thanksgiving throughout Christendom. In 787 Charlemagne set forth his first legislation in the famous *Capitulatio de partibus Saxoniae*, in which Christianity was riveted firmly upon the conquered race and all heathen practices forbidden. But still another revolt in 792 had to be answered by extensive deportations of the population into Frankish territory. Indeed, it was not until the end of the century that the union of the Saxon tribes with the Frankish Kingdom and the establishment of the Christian Church among the Saxons were accomplished facts, the validity of which could no longer be shaken.

In presenting the barbaric element in this missionary episode we must not forget, in conclusion, a redeeming feature supplied by a really Christian leader.

One of the few protests recorded against the royal policy of military and legislative coercion was uttered by Alcuin of York who was active at the court of Charlemagne after 793

[34] Eigilis, *Vita Sturmi*, c. 22.

and who died at Tours in 804. In the autumn of 796 Alcuin wrote to Meganfrid the king's chamberlain, "If the easy yoke and the light burden of Christ had been preached to this most hard race, the Saxons, with as great insistence as the rendering of tithes was required and the legal penalties for the very smallest details, it may be that they would not have abhorred the sacrament of baptism." "Let the teachers of the faith," he adds, "preach, not prey [*sint praedicatores, non praedatores.*]." [35] Earlier in the same year he had expressed similar views when writing to his friend Arno, Archbishop of Salzburg, who had been appointed to accompany a Frankish expedition among the Avars. "Be a preacher of piety," he warns, "not an exactor of tithes; for the freshly converted soul is to be fed with the milk of apostolic piety until it grows, strengthens, and becomes strong enough to receive solid food. Tithes, it is said, have subverted the faith of the Saxons. Why should we place on the neck of the ignorant a yoke which neither we nor our brethren have been able to bear?" [36] Sometime after May 796, when Charlemagne had subjugated the Huns, Alcuin wrote to him in much the same strain, "Now let your most wise and God-pleasing piety provide for the new people pious preachers, of honest life, learned in sacred science, imbued with evangelical precepts, intent in their preaching on the examples of the holy apostles, who were wont to minister milk — that is gentle precepts — to their hearers who were beginners in the faith. . . . Let your most holy piety take into wise consideration whether it is well to impose upon an ignorant race, at the beginning of the faith, the yoke of tithes, so that they shall be fully exacted from house to house. It is worth considering whether the apostles . . . required the exaction of tithes or anywhere demanded them." [37] Three years later Alcuin repeated the same ideas in another letter to the king. "Let peace be made with that wicked people [the Saxons], if that can be done. Let threats be to some extent relaxed,

[35] *M. G. H. Epistolae*, vol. IV, Ep. 111.
[36] *Ibid.*, Ep. 107. Translation from Browne's Alcuin, p. 287.
[37] *Ibid.*, Ep. 110. Browne's Alcuin, pp. 287 f.

so that men may not be hardened. . . . Some time ago I spoke to your piety about the exaction of tithes: that it is decidedly better to abstain from the exaction . . . until the faith has got its roots fixed in the hearts." [38]

But Alcuin was deeply concerned not simply with the question of tithes. The whole system of sudden conversion by force, though he could do little to change it, was plainly of doubtful value in his eyes. He urged Charlemagne, in dealing with the Avars, not to baptize adults until they had first been carefully taught, lest the mere baptism of the body, while the soul remained in ignorance, should profit nothing. And in a letter to Arno of Salzburg, about to preach among the Huns, he warns him of the evil results among the Saxons who had not been properly grounded in the faith. "Apart from faith," he asks, "of what use is baptism? . . . Faith must come voluntarily and not of necessity. How can a man be compelled to believe what he does not believe? A man can be coerced into baptism, but he cannot be coerced into faith." [39] These noble sentences form but one passage in a letter from a scholar to a bishop; they had no effect upon Charlemagne; the simple truth they embody has never been wholly accepted by the Christian Church; yet to have uttered them in the eighth century confers upon Alcuin an imperishable distinction.

The forcible conversion of the Saxons was achieved during the reign of one ruler. Though characterized by brutality and violence, it was a process of no long duration and had, at worst, the merit of being successful. The "conversion" of the Wends, however, was a long drawn out agony that lasted for over two centuries.

The numerous Slavic tribes inhabiting the wide region of forests and swamp lands bounded on the west by the

[38] M. G. H. *Epistolae*, vol. IV, Ep. 174. Browne's Alcuin, pp. 193 f.

[39] *Ibid.*, Ep. 113. Much the same position was taken by Thomas Aquinas nearly four centuries later. "Among unbelievers," he writes, "there are some who have never received the faith, such as the heathen and the Jews: and these are by no means to be compelled to the faith . . . because to believe depends on the will . . . even if [the faithful] were to conquer them . . . they should leave them free to believe, if they will." *Summa Theologica*, II, 2. Q. 10, Art. 8.

Elbe and the Saale and on the east by the Oder were called "Wends" by the Germans.[40] During Charlemagne's reign there had been frequent border warfare between Franks and Wends, with raiding expeditions on both sides; and after his time the Saxon nobles had continued this intermittent fighting, entirely with the aim of private plunder. The official policy of Charlemagne, however, had been essentially defensive. The Wends he regarded not as subjects to be subdued and Christianized, but as foreigners; and for a century, under his successors, this defensive policy was maintained. It was not until the later years of Henry I (919–936) that the subjugation of the Wends became a matter of national concern, to be pursued by systematic offensive measures. The struggle which then began, combining conquest and Christianization, was prolonged and embittered for many generations by the religious tenacity of the Wends and by the rancorous hatred which prevailed between the two contending peoples. Religion was highly developed among the Wends and fostered by an influential priestly caste. An equally deep-seated factor, even more devastating in its results, was the utter contempt of the Franks and Saxons for their Wendish enemy and the responsive loathing of the Wends for their German conquerors. Franks and Saxons, though frequently at war in earlier times, had respected each other and were quick to make friends when the fight was over. But the fact that the Germans despised the Wends and the Wends detested the Germans made their struggles peculiarly savage and ruthless, retarded for centuries the process of assimilation, and enormously exaggerated all the natural difficulties of missionary work.

Under the emperors Henry I and Otto I conquest and ecclesiastical organization proceeded together. As the historian J. W. Thompson has put it, "Precisely as Charlemagne had utilized the administrative system of the Church to extirpate the Saxon tribal organization, so the apparatus

[40] The fullest treatment of the Wends is to be found in Hauck, vol. III, and in R. Wagner-Schwerin, *Die Wendenzeit*. For an account in English, see J. W. Thompson, *Feudal Germany*.

of the German Church was now imposed upon the subjugated Wends in order to crush them." Beyond the Elbe bishoprics arose, their seats "half houses of God, half fortresses." Everywhere the motives of the Church were largely material, and missionary zeal was subordinated to the hunger for land and the appetite for rich endowments.

During a violent and successful revolt of the Wends lasting from 983 to 986 the work of Otto the Great suffered blows from which it did not recover for more than a century, and the missionary organization which he had created was in large measure ruined. In the course of the reigns of Conrad II and Henry III, a period covering the years 1024 to 1056, there was repeated the same familiar story of raids and reprisals and of two rebellions suppressed with a ruthless severity which did the cause of Christianity no good and merely hardened the bitter opposition of the Wends. The archdiocese of Magdeburg, created by Otto to pursue the conversion of the Wends, neglected all its opportunities. But its bishops could hardly be blamed. In the eyes of the Wends — and perhaps in their own — they were only officials of conquering emperors. The imperial Church, wholly identified with the hated German rule, no longer had the will or the power to carry out bold and persistent missionary work.

Even at the beginning of the twelfth century heathenism still prevailed throughout Wendish territory, so meager were the results of nearly two hundred years of forceful methods. Broadly speaking, when the kingdom in Germany had been powerful the spread of the Church under its leadership and the acceptance of Christianity by the Wends had been presented as a demand by the state to be enforced by means of the civil power. The more violently effective were the political and military methods the greater the rebellious resentment engendered among the conquered and the more damage done from the religious point of view. On the other hand, whenever the legislative and administrative activity of the kingdom began to weaken, the furtherance of missionary work was left to the bishops who, for lack of royal control and protection, ceased their activity. The consequence was that no one assumed responsibility and the ecclesiastical machine came to a standstill. In other words, when force was vigorously applied it generally had just the wrong effect, producing violent pagan reactions. And when, through changes of personnel or of policy, there came intervals of quiescence, the Church had too little missionary vitality of its own to pursue any methods more religiously effective. It is small wonder, then, that there was little to show for two centuries of fluctuating activity which had been either unsuccessfully violent or unsuccessfully feeble.

The last concerted attempt to force Christianity upon the Wends took shape under Lothar in the Wendish Crusade of 1147, a campaign promoted by the fervent eloquence of St. Bernard of Clairvaux. Everywhere the clergy united in urging upon people as well as nobles the duty of joining the crusade, with promises of forgiveness of sins to all who shared in it. Bohemians and Poles combined with Saxons in contributing to the host. Yet, considering the forces involved, the crusade was a failure.

Having wrought desolation over wide areas of Wendish territory, the crusaders had achieved this much success — the Wendish chief Niclot submitted to the Saxon leaders and agreed that he and his people would accept Christianity and pay a yearly tribute to Henry of Saxony. But the chronicler Helmold is undoubtedly right in asserting that the Wends had been made more hostile than ever by the crusade and less amenable than ever to the genuine acceptance of Christianity. Princely promises and a few baptisms made no real difference in missionary prospects, and after 1147 it became quite evident that "the territory of the Wends would not become Christian so long as it remained Wendish. Only through German immigration could Christianity be established."

Indeed, the rest of the tragic story is simply that of the slow expulsion of the remaining Wends from their former

lands and the Christianization of Wendish territory not by
the conversion of the Wends but by the intrusion of Christian
Germans. After the destructive year of the crusade began
the final period of relentless organization and expansion. In
the central area under the Margrave Albert the Bear the
Wends were driven into remote corners by extensive German
immigration, the see cities of Havelberg and Brandenburg
were restored; and churches, rebuilt or newly founded,
rapidly increased in number. But most of the surviving
Wends would have nothing to do with Christianity and the
few who had been baptized took no part in church life.
Further north, Henry the Lion completed the work of
systematic subjugation, ending the last sign of rebellion in
1162. Here, too, it was the active immigration of German
settlers which made this region finally Christian. At the
end of the twelfth century Christianity was at last victorious
in the whole wide region between the Elbe and the Oder.
Yet with fragmentary exceptions the Wends had never been
Christianized. Clinging tenaciously to their pagan faith,
they had, for the most part, been either exterminated or expelled. The missionary method of force, never before pursued in Europe with so few mitigating features, had worked
itself out to the limit. The land was at last Christian, but
the great bulk of its inhabitants were no longer Wends.

The activity of Bishop Otto of Bamberg in founding the
Church in Pomerania offers one of the most notable instances
in missionary history of evangelization under political
auspices. For here the religious and secular strands in the
process were clearly interwoven to an unusual degree, so that
neither element was secondary or negligible and each appeared dependent upon the other for the success achieved.
Though his work, in point of time, precedes the final conquest of the Wends and the campaigns of the Teutonic
knights in Prussia, it may well conclude our survey of
"kings and missionaries," because it exemplifies all three of
the types we have considered. And it deserves a fairly de-

tailed description since it is an unfamiliar story based on
sources unusually full and reliable.

The area inhabited by the Slavic tribes known as Pomeranians was the valley of the lower Oder and the territory
eastward toward the Vistula. On the west lay the Wendish
regions, largely Germanized in Otto's time, and to the east
was the kingdom of Poland with its capital at Gnesen.
Separated from Germany by the Wends, the Pomeranians
had been subject for some two centuries to invasion and
temporary control by the Danes and the Poles. But it was
Polish expansion which had proved the more consistent and
aggressive and which ultimately provided the setting of
Otto's work. Duke Boleslav I of Poland (Boleslav Chrobry,
992–1025) had forced the Pomeranians to recognize Polish
sovereignty and had followed up his victories with the first
missionary attempts in Pomerania. The ensuing loss of
Polish control, however, ended Christian activity, and when
aggression, often renewed, began once again in the time of
Boleslav III (1102–1138), Pomerania was still heathen territory untouched by Christo-German civilization. After a
series of campaigns between 1107 and 1120, Boleslav III,
at the cost of wide devastation and frightful slaughter,
succeeded in subjugating western Pomerania, took possession of its capital Stettin, and reduced to vassalage its ruler
Duke Wartislav. Part of the terms of peace agreed to by the
duke and his followers in 1120 was the acceptance of Christianity by the Pomeranians. Here we see the element of
force exerted by a foreign invader.

Having accomplished all that physical power could contribute to the Christianization of his new possessions, Boleslav tried to find missionaries who would make potential conversion actual. Since he was unable to obtain them among
his own clergy, he turned to the celebrated German bishop,
Otto of Bamberg, then about sixty years of age and at the
height of his prosperous career. The choice was natural, for
close relations existed between the bishop and the Polish
court where Otto had spent some years in earlier life under

Duke Vladislav, as chaplain to the latter's wife who was a sister of the emperor Henry IV. "At length [Boleslav] decided to invite to undertake this task Otto, the bishop of Bamberg, whose fame had spread abroad throughout his kingdom and whom in his early youth his own father had held dear. He therefore sent ambassadors and gifts and wrote a letter" in which, we are told, he promised to provide "all expenses and companions for the journey, both interpreters and assistant priests and whatever else is needed." [41] After many months devoted to negotiation, preparation, and the securing of papal approval, Otto set out at the head of his expedition in May, 1124.

The situation which he was to encounter in Pomerania was at once favorable and unfavorable; and for both factors the forcible subjugation of Pomerania by the Poles may be held responsible. On the one hand was the suppressed resentment engendered by the long and hopeless struggle of the people against their Polish adversaries. Christianity was the religion of their bitterest enemies and was likewise identified with the alien Germans who had for centuries oppressed the neighboring Wends. Fortified by racial hatred the Pomeranians, as a whole, were still pagan, and their powerful priesthood knew how to exploit the nationalistic spirit in defence of the ancient religion. But these were only the more obvious features that confronted Otto. Less easy to note but ultimately decisive were other facts. Nearly two centuries of warfare, culminating in complete Polish success, had not merely roused antagonism. They had gone far to break down moral as well as physical resistance. The people had lost confidence in their old gods, and heathenism had been so much weakened that it was more nearly ready to collapse than outside observers realized. The time was ripe for the coming change.

That change, indeed, had already begun, and its progress was everywhere furthered by the fact that many Pomeranians, especially among the ruling classes, had become

[41] Herbordus, II, 6. The date is 1122 or 1123.

Christian before the arrival of Otto. Their relations with
Germans and Poles, either at home or when travelling
abroad, had no doubt moved them to take this step so certain to improve their standing. Duke Wartislav of Pomerania had been baptized at Merseburg in his youth; his wife
was a Christian; and not a few of his followers, though they
had abandoned the practice of Christianity, had once been
believers. In the towns, too, some of the local leaders were
Christians. Both of these factors — the breakdown of pagan
morale and the growing number of prominent Christians —
had made possible the pledge of 1120 that the Pomeranians
would accept Christianity. From the tactical point of view
this agreement in the peace treaty was of the greatest value
to Otto. In the vernacular of today it gave him a "talking
point" in appealing to a people whose leaders had made a
definite promise on their behalf. Whatever the promise
might be worth, the fact that it had been given was an advantage for which Otto was indebted to the Duke of Poland,
an advantage which largely determined his mode of approach and partly explains his remarkable success.

The narrative of Otto's first missionary journey of
1124–25, as recorded in full detail by his three biographers,
is a story of exceptional interest; but we can only sum-
marize it briefly with an eye to the assistance rendered to
the bishop by the rulers of Poland and Pomerania and their
subordinates.

The original plan of Boleslav, it would seem, had contemplated a Polish expedition under the leadership of Otto,
but the mission which actually set out in May, 1124, was a
German mission with Polish support. Otto took with him
about twenty clergy of his own diocese and numerous servants, together with an ample supply of provisions, church
utensils, vestments, books and presents. After travelling
through Bohemia and Silesia, Otto was met near the border of
Poland by messengers of Duke Boleslav with whom he
journeyed to the capital at Gnesen. There he was received
with great reverence by the duke and his chief nobles who

entertained him for a week or more. Before he departed Boleslav provided him with a military escort of sixty soldiers commanded by the count Paul who was to serve as the duke's representative with the view of heightening Otto's prestige and emphasizing the patronage under which he worked. "He collected a long line of chariots and four-horse carriages to carry the provisions and all the sacred vessels of the bishop and the money also which was provided by his country with great liberality, as he contemplated that the bishop would not need to labor or to spend his own money, but desired to secure by his own expenditure the whole merit arising from his journey. The duke also gave the bishop three chaplains, who were with him, to assist in preaching the word, and a certain centurion named Paulicius, a strenuous and orthodox man, who was fitted by his natural gift of eloquence to act as a popular speaker." [42]

The bishop's coming having been announced by messengers, Duke Wartislav "met him in a town called Zitarigroda and received him with honor as a messenger of God. Otto offered to him the peace of Christ and, in accordance with his custom, presented gifts, namely a bishop's seat covered with an [episcopal] mantle and a costly dorsal together with other gifts, in order that by endowing him with temporal goods he might the more easily incite him to the love of heavenly things." [43] And before Otto set forth on his journey into the mission field Wartislav left with him guides and armed guards "and gave orders that in every district . . . throughout the whole of Pomerania liberal hospitality should be provided for the bishop." [44] Thus commissioned and protected by the two dukes Otto was prepared to begin his task.

The general policy which Otto followed in dealing with the inhabitants of the various towns which he visited was to put to the people and their leaders the definite question whether or not they would accept baptism. Even if not specially mentioned, it was understood on both sides that the question

[42] Herbordus, II, 9. Robinson's translation.
[43] Ebo, II, 4.   [44] Herbordus, II, 12.

was natural and relevant in view of the general Pomeranian pledge of four years before. In that sense and to that extent he took advantage of political conditions and depended on political power. If he met with a favorable response, brief instruction and baptism followed. Otherwise he proceeded to public preaching and negotiation with leading citizens. Since he was accompanied by Polish and Pomeranian soldiers and was a recognized emissary of both Boleslav and Wartislav, political coercion then became even more obvious. And in still more difficult cases he was even ready to appeal to the Duke of Poland.

Reaching Pyritz early in June, "the bishop sent to the camp Paul and the messengers of Duke Boleslav. These saluted the chief men in the name of the dukes and announced that the bishop had been sent by the dukes to declare to them the Christian faith and religion. With their authority they commanded and endeavored to persuade the people to listen reverently and respectfully, and they further stated that the bishop was a man of rank and wealth in his own country and possessed resources sufficient to supply his needs in a foreign land, and that he sought nothing and needed nothing, but had come in order to promote their salvation and not for the sake of gain. They bade them to remember their pledged word and to be mindful of the divine vengeance and of the recent destruction that had come upon the land, lest they should a second time arouse the divine wrath. They pointed out that the whole world lived under Christian laws and that they could not by themselves withstand the whole world." [45]

Here we may note that the negotiation was entrusted to the Polish count Paul, that (if we trust the report) he made specific reference to the "pledged word" of the people, and that the "recent destruction" to which he alluded as "divine vengeance" was really the work of Duke Boleslav. These political motives and methods were effective at Pyritz; the people submitted, and hundreds were baptized.

[45] Herbordus, II, 14.

Toward the end of the month the mission reached the town of Kammin, near the mouth of the Oder, where Duke Wartislav had a residence and where his wife lived. Partly through her influence their success was so great that they remained for three months teaching the people and baptizing more than thirty-five hundred. During their stay Wartislav arrived for a visit. Many of his soldiers were instructed and baptized, and he himself publicly renounced his twenty-four concubines and persuaded some of his subordinates to follow his example. Before leaving he donated several farms and other property for the support of a priest and provided a certain Domislav and his two sons to act as ambassadors and guides.

The next move was across the mouth of the Oder to the island of Wollin where the party met with violent opposition and were practically besieged for a week in a residence of the duke which served them as an asylum of refuge. "We remained there," says Herbordus' informant, "on the other side of the marsh which surrounded the town for fifteen days, waiting to see if the people would come to a better state of mind. Meanwhile our companions went to and fro between us and them, and their head men came to us and excused themselves by laying the blame for the tumult upon the stupid and worthless section of the people. The bishop then conversed with them concerning the Christian faith and endeavored indirectly to exhort and persuade them. He made mention also of the name and power of the Duke of Poland and suggested that the insult offered to us would tend to his injury and that some evil might befall them in consequence, unless perchance their conversion should intervene. They said that they would take advice, and having gone back to their own people, they discussed these matters over and over again and at length arrived at a unanimous decision, namely, that in regard to this proposal they would do whatever the inhabitants of Stettin did, for they said that this city was the oldest and most renowned in Pomerania and was the mother of cities and that it would not be right for them to permit the observance of a new religion unless this observance had first been confirmed by its authority." [46]

Since even the menace of force had served only to postpone the decision of the townsfolk, the expedition was obliged to move up the Oder to Stettin, taking with them as guide a Christian citizen of Wollin. In Stettin, too, the inhabitants were openly hostile and seemed proof against both the preaching of the bishop and the threats of Paul and the other ambassadors. "As all continued obstinate we effected nothing, although we remained there two months, and even more. As this long and useless delay was a cause of distress to us, a proposal was made that we should send messengers to the Duke of Poland to inquire what orders he would give us, whether we were to remain there or to return, and what he thought of the opposition offered by the inhabitants of the town. When this proposal became known to the citizens they were afraid, but asked nevertheless that messengers be sent, and said that their own messengers would coöperate with them on the understanding that if they should obtain from the duke a lasting peace and a reduction of the tribute, and if this should be confirmed in writing in the presence of their own and the bishop's messengers, they would then of their own free will regard with favor the Christian laws." [47] While awaiting the results of this direct appeal to temporal power, Otto busied himself with evangelism and had already begun to meet with success before the return of the embassy.

"While these things were happening in the town Paul and the messengers alike of the pagans and Christians arrived from the Duke of Poland and, having accomplished that which had been commanded them, they brought back a letter from the king which read as follows: 'Boleslav, by the favor of almighty God, Duke of Poland, and the enemy of all pagans, to the Pomeranian race and to the people of Stettin who remain true to their pledges and promises, offers firm peace and lasting friendship, but to those who do not observe them, slaughter and burning and lasting hostility. If I de-

[46] Herbordus, II, 25.   [47] Herbordus, II, 26.

sired an occasion to attack you I could be justly indignant because I perceive that you have not kept faith but have gone back therefrom and have not received in befitting manner my lord and father Bishop Otto, who is worthy of all honor and reverence and whose fame is spread amongst all peoples and races, who has moreover been sent from God by our instrumentality to promote your salvation; neither have ye been obedient to his teaching according to the fear of God. All these things constitute a strong indictment against you, but my representatives and your own, who are honorable and prudent men, have intervened on your behalf, and more especially the bishop himself who is staying with you and who is your evangelist and apostle. I have judged it right therefore to accede to their advice and petition, and have decided to lighten your burden of servitude and tribute so that ye may with greater readiness take upon you the yoke of Christ. The whole land of the Pomeranian peoples is to pay as a public tribute to the Duke of Poland, whoever he may be, only 300 silver marks year by year. If war assail him they are to assist him in the following manner. Every nine heads of households shall equip for the war the tenth with arms and money and shall meanwhile carefully provide for his household. If ye keep this agreement and conform to the Christian religion, ye shall obtain peace from my outstretched hand, and the joy of eternal life, and on all occasions ye shall receive as friends and allies the protection and support of the people of Poland.' An assembly was thereupon held at which these statements were read out in the presence of the people and the chiefs, who eagerly took the oaths, and submitted themselves to gospel teaching." [48]

Though we cannot assume that we have here the actual words of the duke, the general purpose and achievements of this mission to Poland are clear. Warning and persuasion might first be tried, but no adverse decision was to be accepted as final without previous appeal to the strong arm of Boleslav. His power, exercised in so conciliatory a fashion,

[48] Herbordus, II, 30.

turned the tide in favor of Christianity. As a result, the people of Wollin, following suit, sent messengers of high rank to recall Otto to their town where he was honorably received and where he spent six weeks or more in baptizing the people.

By this time it was about the first of February, 1125, and Otto had begun to receive messages begging him to return to Bamberg. But before he set his face homeward he devoted a few weeks to visiting several towns east of the Oder — Klötikow, Kolberg, and Belgard. Ebo's account of the stay at Clodona (Klötikow) gives a striking picture of the effect of Boleslav's campaigns and of the spirit in which the subjugated inhabitants accepted Christianity. "At Clodona," we read, "he baptized many Pomeranians who had returned from the islands of the sea where they had hidden in fear of the duke Boleslav. For the duke Boleslav, who was distinguished for his piety, and his devotion to God and the worshippers of God, was deservedly harsh, and implacable towards idolaters and those accused of crimes. He was wont year after year to raise a large army and to devastate the lands of the pagans in order that, through fear of the sword, they might be brought into subjection to the Christian faith. And when this was accomplished by the instrumentality of Otto, war was changed to peace and all came out of the hiding-places where they had been concealed, and, having accepted the safety which was secured to them by the good bishop, obtained the grace of baptism. This helped to delay the preacher of the truth and kept him for some time at Clodona. When all his business had been accomplished, he set out for Belgard and afterwards for Kolberg." [49]

"On our return from this country we accomplished our journey with the help of our father, the Duke of Poland. May the Lord Jesus in the day of acknowledgment repay him all the good that he showed to us. For so much affection and kindness was manifested towards us that, as we were stationed in Pomerania in winter time, this excellent man sent us winter garments suitable for the bishop and for each

[49] Ebo, II, 18.

individual person, whether clergy, soldiers, or shield-bearers. As we had now accomplished the task to which he had himself called us, he received all of us on our return as beloved sons, and bestowed fitting honors upon the bishop and all the others, leaving no one unrewarded." [50]

By the end of March, 1125, the expedition had returned in safety to Bamberg. The Pomeranian Church had been founded. As our narrative has clearly indicated, the previous use of force had created a situation favorable to the success of Otto and potential force in reserve made his task easier. But it must not be forgotten that the memory of past violence and the fear of its recurrence would not in themselves have been sufficient even for the degree of Christianization which was accomplished. The failure of mere power exerted against the Wends had proved that over and over again. The circumstances surrounding Otto's work were favorable only because he made the right use of them. In the first place, his own strong preference on all occasions was for winning voluntary consent, and Ebo quotes him as saying, "God does not desire forced but voluntary service." And not only at this point did he differ from the accepted methods of his day. By being obviously self-supporting and by exacting nothing material from the people whom he approached he allayed the mistrust so often roused among the Wends by Christian Germans. In actual practice he carried out Alcuin's advice to Bishop Arno "to preach and not to prey." By resolutely confining himself to peaceful means, by meeting every situation in the spirit of conciliation and goodwill, and by the contagious effect of his own impressive personality he achieved for the Church a victory which lesser men would have missed.

The second mission of Otto to Pomerania, organized three years later, was carried out under changed conditions and different auspices. Since the bishop's return to Bamberg in 1125, Lothar, the Duke of Saxony, had become emperor and had begun to extend the power of Germany among the Wends. The Western Pomeranians under Wartislav, revolt-

[50] Herbordus, II, 42.

ing against the power of Boleslav, had broken their oath of fidelity to him, and he was preparing to launch a punitive campaign against them. Moreover, as a result of this uprising, several of the leading towns had experienced a relapse into paganism, and the fruits of Otto's work were imperilled. He resolved, accordingly, upon a second mission. But with Boleslav and Wartislav at sword's points he could hardly plan for the same method of approach as before. He determined instead to make his expedition wholly German and to advance upon Pomerania from the German side with German protection. Lothar was ready enough to grant his approval and patronage, for he was deeply concerned to advance the cause of Christianity among the pagan Slavs and realized the political advantage of promoting its spread under German auspices and at the expense of Polish prestige. In addition to the aid supplied by the emperor, Otto obtained further support from Albert the Bear, Margrave of Brandenburg, who had shown great zeal in Christianizing his own subjects in the neighboring Slavic regions. The help afforded to Otto by these rulers, however, was largely that of political and moral prestige, for no military escort was furnished him and there is no record in the biographies of financial and material contributions. He appears to have depended on the rich resources of his own church lands; yet the expedition was conducted on so large and costly a scale that we can safely assume that some measure of practical aid was supplied by Lothar, of the sort that had previously been given by Boleslav. At all events, there was far less evidence, on this mission, of political and military power either directly displayed or indirectly employed.

On April 18, 1128, Otto set out northward from Bamberg with a large retinue of clergy and servants. At Halle and elsewhere he gathered provisions and other supplies in such quantities that by the time his expedition entered Leuticia, in Wendish territory, it consisted of fifty chariots and four horse wagons. After an arduous journey partly by boat on the Elbe and Havel and partly across country the mission arrived at Demmin on the borders of Leuticia and Pomerania. There they met Duke Wartislav who had just returned from a plundering expedition among the neighboring Lyutitzi and who conducted the party on a three days' journey by boat down the river Peene to the island of Usedom which was to be their headquarters.

"The duke then appointed a general conference of the leading men of his kingdom to be held in [Usedom] on the festivity of Pentecost. When the chief men of the town of Demmin and of the other towns were come together he urged them with words of wisdom to take upon themselves the yoke of the Christian faith." He dwelt upon the dignity and saintliness of Otto whom he described as "beloved of our lord the invincible King Lothar," and ended with this menacing reminder; "If [Bishop Otto] suffer at your hands any trouble or distress, our lord the king will speedily come with an army and will blot you and your land out of existence." [51] Since the biographer Ebo depended on information obtained from the priest Udalric who accompanied Otto on this journey, we are justified in regarding the account of this appeal as essentially reliable. The story in Herbordus, however, includes a long speech by Wartislav which is undoubtedly fictitious. Yet part of it so perfectly summarizes the medieval conception of the relation between ruler and people in the matter of religious conversion that it deserves quotation. "It is for us who are reputed to be, and are, the chiefs and elders to consult our own dignity and to give our consent in a worthy and pious manner so that the people who are subject to us may be taught by our example. For whatever sanctity or integrity in the sight of God or man is to be sought after, I think that it is more right and comely that it should pass from the head to the members than from the members to the head. In the primitive Church, as we have heard, the Christian religion began with the people and with common persons and spread to the middle classes and at length affected the great chiefs of the world. Let us change the order of the primitive Church

[51] Ebo, III, 6.

and let it begin with us who are the chiefs and, passing on from us to the middle classes by an easy progress, let the sanctifying influence of the divine religion enlighten the whole people and nation." [52]

The fruits of this important conference were reaped not only in Usedom itself but soon afterward at Wolgast and Gützkow, westward on the mainland, where Otto brought about the destruction of heathen temples and the reception of large numbers into the Church.

These successes in western Pomerania had been achieved without the aid of the Polish duke, but they could hardly have been maintained had Otto not been willing to negotiate with him on behalf of the Pomeranians. For, as we have seen, Boleslav was on the point of restoring his authority in that area by military force. In fear of his coming attack the leading citizens of Usedom and the nearby towns begged Otto, as their best friend, to intercede for them with his former patron Boleslav. "I am myself ready," the bishop replied, "to lay down my life on your behalf: only devote your attention to the religion which ye have learned. I and my companions will go to the Duke of Poland and with God's help, will induce him to abandon his intention of making war." Determined to save his new flock from the horrors of a devastating invasion, Otto travelled all the way to Poland where he had a long interview with the indignant duke. Boleslav was extremely reluctant to "lose face" by calling off his expedition; but the force of Otto's personal appeal and the fact that he stood under the protection of the emperor combined to persuade the duke. He consented to spare Pomerania provided that Duke Wartislav would come to him in person, beg for pardon, and renew his oath of fidelity. Wartislav complied with this demand, and after three days of negotiation the two dukes were reconciled and gave mutual pledges to maintain the peace. Some weeks later when Otto, after a series of contests with the pagan priests, had succeeded in reëstablishing Christianity at Stettin, the citizens

[52] Herbordus, III, 3.

of that town, who were on bad terms with Wartislav, begged that the bishop would intervene to end the dispute. Otto went at once to see the duke at Kammin and speedily brought about a reconciliation. The remarkable power of Otto over these two rulers could hardly have been more convincingly displayed than by these incidents. They remind us that throughout his brief missionary career it was he who used them rather than they who used him.

Otto's second missionary tour, limited as it was to the island of Usedom and the neighboring towns, added little to the extent of the Church. It was abruptly ended by an urgent summons from Lothar, commanding Otto to return as quickly as possible. The need of the emperor for his counsel and assistance is cited by Ebo as the chief reason for the recall; but it is likely that Lothar may have looked askance at the negotiation with Boleslav which bade fair to reëstablish the authority of the Polish duke over the whole of Pomerania. Obedient to his sovereign's order, Otto left for home and arrived in Bamberg before Christmas, 1128, seven months after his departure.

Even so brief a summary of Otto's many months of work is enough to remind us of the numerous points of resemblance between such medieval movements and their modern counterparts. The entrance among a people of foreign missionaries coming with a certain prestige from a more advanced civilization; the leadership of local chiefs, conscious of various material as well as religious benefits to be derived from conversion; the interchange of views with neighboring communities; the variety of response, varying from prompt acquiescence to settled hostility; the group decisions followed by wholesale baptism; the instruction provided both before and after baptism; the arrangements for future church guidance and nurture; the gradual building up of a native church — all these features have long been familiar outside Pomerania. The two clearest points of difference, of course, are the presence of political and military force hovering in the background and the favorable fact that the greater part of Europe was already Christian and that the Pomeranians were only being asked to join the vast majority.

The wide variety of examples which we have examined will have made clear how large was the share of rulers in the conversion of northern Europe. To put it in other words, group movements to Christianity were plainly characteristic of the expansion of the Church in Europe during the Middle Ages. Whether peacefully or forcibly promoted they took the form of mass conversions. When the process was steady and peaceful — as it usually was — the change, as we have seen, was due to following a recognized leader, local or foreign, in a matter which was primarily his to decide. When the leader was merely foreign and quite unrecognized, the process had to be forcible and the change should be traced not to the social organization of the time but to the conqueror's mere power — a type of conversion which of course may appear at any period, as among the Muslim invaders of India or the Spanish invaders in Central America. In each and every case, moreover, the change was aided not only by the form of political organism but by the type of religion superseded, which was uniformly a tribal or state nature religion.

Whether such a method of conversion be the best is a further question perhaps hardly worth discussing in the abstract since it was the only method which, at that time and place, would have resulted in conversion. Individual conversion, one by one, each representing a genuine change of heart, may well be viewed as more in harmony with the essential meaning of Christianity. It was characteristic of the first two centuries of our era and it has been characteristic of missions for the past century in such high civilizations as those of China and Japan. But northern Europe could not have been won in that way, certainly not in the period in which its conversion was achieved. Group conversions are not likely to occur except where social and religious traditions make them normal and natural; and if they are normal and natural they are to be welcomed as such and not condemned by reference to alien standards. The first and simplest lesson, then, which the modern missionary can learn from the Middle Ages is that, for better or worse, most of his ancestors were converted in large groups for good reasons, and that when similar causes reappear elsewhere they will produce similar effects. In other words, the real problem is not why group movements have occurred or whether they will recur, but what to do with them when we meet them.

That question, however, was not a serious problem for the medieval Catholic Church, for its conception of conversion, of Christianity, and of the Church was congenial to mass movements and conducive to handling them with untroubled conscience and without sensitive misgivings. It was not difficult for the Church in that age to adapt itself to the situation which confronted it, since that was the very period when the corporate aspect of Christianity was most strongly emphasized. Not simply within the religious and social life of paganism was the individual subordinated to the group. Within the Church itself the same was true. That Church was no voluntary association of mature and instructed believers; it was the great Ark of Salvation, an august institution dispensing the sacraments as the only means of salvation. There was no practical distinction between Christianity and the Church, and men thought in terms not of individual religious experience but of submission to corporate authority, obedience to simple laws, and the reception of sacramental grace. No readjustment of method or belief, therefore, was required to admit whole masses by baptism. The readiness of these converts to submit to baptism was *prima facie* evidence of a sufficient faith, the rite itself saved them from the eternal penalties of original sin, and their incorporation into the Body of Christ was regarded as the necessary beginning of a slow process of nurture in the light of which the crude initial stages of development were to be interpreted. The pagans and their rulers, Christian missionaries and Christian monarchs, bishops and popes — all were alike in thinking of religion as corporate and objective. Each side, therefore, understood the other, and the Church, in consequence, found its traditional attitude and technique adequate to meet the situation.

Though the king and the missionary as partners were united by these common convictions, there was not a little variation in the type of relationship that existed between them. Sometimes the missionary was the dominating figure and the attitude of the monarch respectfully acquiescent, as with Otto and Wartislav. Sometimes the two were strong fellow-workers on a footing of equality, each in his sphere, as with Aidan and Oswald or Boniface and Charles Martel. On other occasions the missionaries were only pawns moved about to suit the masterful tactics of a sovereign, as with Willehad and Charlemagne or the German bishops during the conquest of the Wends. `The general tendency from the sixth century onward, despite marked exceptions, was for the monarch to develop from a patron to a master and for the missionary to decline from an independent initiator to an agent in the extension of royal plans.

This evolution, by which the emphasis shifted ever more markedly to the political side, supplies one reason for the increasing readiness to use physical force, or to speak more accurately, for the growing fusion of political and missionary expansion by military means. The whole of England was converted without resort to force. Though Willibrord and Boniface were indirectly aided by Frankish conquests, their own labors were of a genuinely evangelistic type. But when we come to Charlemagne and the Saxons, to the "conversion" or gradual extermination of the Wends and Prussians, and to the systematic Christianizing activity of the Olafs in Norway, we find force not merely vaguely in reserve but openly exerted. Broadly speaking, that is, so far as rulers controlled the process — or so far as missionary ends were only incidental to political — the strong arm of the state had full scope. On the other hand, so far as the missionary was the central figure and free to follow his own path, the element of compulsion was slight or wholly lacking.

Such a generalization, however, though true as far as it

goes, omits another factor which accounts more fully for the contrast between peaceful and violent methods. As we review the facts it seems to be true that the use of military power to serve ends that were at least partly missionary was confined to cases in which Christian rulers were conquering some alien race. Kings did not campaign against their own people to make them Christian. That would have proved both intolerable and unsuccessful. It would have lacked the leverage of any popular motive or general support. So viewed, there was no opportunity or inducement for such crusading in England. Even in Norway the use of brute violence was too occasional and local to deserve the name of campaign. When we turn, however, to the history of the Saxons, Wends, and Prussians, the psychological situation is utterly different. Conquest once determined on for political reasons by a Christian state, religious purposes were so inextricably intertwined with military that the submission demanded of a heathen race must include surrender to Church no less than to king. And it is no accident that in such campaigns the missionaries, where in evidence at all, were often hardly more than camp-followers.

The social organization of pagan peoples, the relation of Church and state in Christian lands, and the Catholic conception of the nature of the Church and its sacraments combined to render inevitable the coöperation of king and missionary. How far the widespread conversion which their methods achieved fell short of Christianization is another and an even longer story.

CHAPTER III

MISSIONS AND MONASTICISM

THE part played by the monastic system in the conversion of northern Europe would be impressive enough if our only evidence were the education of the leading missionaries, for nearly all of them, as we have seen, were products of the monastery. Nowhere else, indeed, could the necessary training and inspiration be provided. But monasteries were not merely points of departure for medieval evangelists. In the opening of every fresh field of advance new monasteries, small and rudimentary at first, sprang up to serve as rallying points for the Christian forces, às homes for the workers, and as centers where native leaders might be developed. And the large institutions in Christian lands continued to perform the invaluable function of home bases for the supply of money, of men, and of spiritual encouragement.

The missionary rôle of monasticism in Ireland and Scotland during the era of Columba was even more dominant than elsewhere and at other times, since the Celtic Church was organized almost wholly on monastic lines. The Christianity of that time and place was monastic Christianity; all the missionaries were monks and all their bases monasteries. As Dowden has written, "The monastery was everywhere the home and seminary of Christian learning, the center of Christian work, and everywhere, as it were, the military base of operations against the powers of heathendom. There is not one name of eminence in the history of Celtic Christianity that is not closely connected with the monastic life." [1] Celtic monasticism was therefore of a peculiar type. Not being merely auxiliary or supplementary to parochial or diocesan organization, it had to cover nearly all the ground there was and to adjust itself to the prevailing social system. For that reason it calls for somewhat fuller description than is demanded by missionary monasticism elsewhere.

[1] J. Dowden, pp. 216 f.

The Celtic monastic church was in one sense a tribal institution. Each one of the great monasteries was a center of family relation and served as a school and asylum for all who were related by blood to the founder or patron. These larger monasteries were thus Christian colonies within the tribe, into which converts might be brought as monks without essentially changing their social position with reference to their tribe or their land. There they found a great ecclesiastical family or community where they were granted not only the religious privileges of worship and education but the social privileges of greater security and the right of sanctuary. This Christian community, moreover, was closely related to the tribal organization, each supporting and reflecting the other. The abbots, for example, were not elected by the brethren in the fashion later customary but succeeded one another by a law similar to that of the tribe. The usual rule in the monasteries was to elect a new abbot from the founder's kin or, if such candidates were lacking, to choose him from some collateral branch. At Iona, for instance, all the early abbots, with one or two exceptions, were strictly limited to a branch of the Tir-Conall family. Furthermore, the monastic community, in return for granting to the tribe the privileges of the sacraments, had a right to demand tithes and first-fruits.[2]

The organization of the monastery at Iona and the life of its monks have been fully described by Reeves on the basis of an examination, line by line, of Adamnan's Life of Columba. As abbot of Iona, writing a century after Columba's death, Adamnan was exceptionally equipped to give a reliable account of a typical Celtic monastery, an account which would apply, in its main features, to other monasteries in Scotland and Ireland in both the sixth and the seventh centuries, for the Columban Church in Scotland was a mission from the Irish Church, and in every respect resembled it.

Iona was essentially a large family of which the abbot was

[2] Skene, vol. II, ch. 2.

the father. He had jurisdiction not only over the monastery itself but over the affiliated monasteries founded by him or his disciples in Ireland and Scotland. These he occasionally visited and regulated, and from him their superiors received their charge. The abbot of Iona, as of many other monasteries, was a presbyter, not a bishop; but there were always bishops connected with the society and subject, by their monastic vow, to the abbot. The bishops were honored as such, and their exclusive power to ordain was respected. But over all the monks, bishops included, the abbot was a supreme autocrat. He could relax or increase discipline, institute a festival, dispense with a fast, give leave for departure, forbid admission to the island, and exert control over all the temporalities. He could even name his successor, giving preference to the founder's kin. In keeping with the family conception of the community, its members were called "brothers" and sometimes "sons of the abbot," though in course of time they came to include not only Irish but also Britons and Saxons. The brothers were divided into three groups. First were the older members of tried devotedness who gave themselves chiefly to the conduct of religious services and to reading and transcribing the Scriptures. Second were the working brothers capable of manual labor in agriculture, domestic service, and manufacture. Third were the younger men and boys under instruction. The total number of monks at Iona in Columba's time is reported to have been one hundred and fifty.

In Columba's monastery there was probably no formal written Rule such as that of Columbanus in France; but definite vows of poverty, celibacy, and obedience were taken by the monks. All property was held in common; marriage, though not uncommon among the secular clergy, was forbidden to the regular; and obedience, limited to things lawful, was strictly observed. In addition to the full members of the community who had taken these vows, there were others who wished to retire from the world without assuming such obligations. These associates might or might

not become full members. Ordinary probationers constituted yet another group awaiting formal admission during
a period of varying length. Enjoying only a temporary connection with the community were the "penitents" — fugi-
tives from justice or others burdened by their sins, who came
to confess and to undergo the penance prescribed by the
abbot. Finally, there were the "guests" — pilgrims, trav-
ellers, or refugees from oppression, for whom hospitable
provision was always made. If they were poor or sick, their
needs were often met, since almsgiving was a virtue greatly
favored and some measure of medical care could be offered.

The economic life of this large community was of course
self-sustaining. The buildings were simple and primitive,
constituting a rude village of huts more like the settlements
of pioneers than the substantial monasteries of a later age.
A large number of detached huts or cells made of wood or of
wattles housed the brethren. Likewise of wood were the
larger buildings — the chapel, the refectory, the kitchen,
the library, the abbot's house, the guest-house, the smithy,
and the carpenter's shop. Around them all was a rampart
of earth or stone. Outside this enclosure were not only other
buildings such as the mill, the granary, the cow-stable, the
barn, and the boat-house, but also the pasture and the fields
for growing corn and vegetables.

The occupations of the community were worship, labor,
and study. Adamnan does not specifically mention the order
of daily services; but it is likely, from references in the lives
of other Celtic saints and from Adamnan's frequent allusions
to the recitation of the Psalter, that the usual canonical
hours were observed, except by the working brethren. The
Eucharist was celebrated on Sundays and feast days. Manual
labor held a large place in the life of the monastery — agriculture, fishing, carpentering, cooking, and the manufacture
of goods for personal and domestic use. More important,
from our point of view, were the activities of study and teaching. One group of the brethren spent most of their time in
study, of which the primary subject was of course the

Scriptures. Though there was usually an official scribe, much attention was devoted by others to the copying of the Scriptures and of service books. Columba himself was a particularly noted scribe. Teaching in the monastic school was a further duty laid upon the more accomplished monks, involving a course of instruction which usually began with the rudiments of reading and writing taught with the Psalms as the material for use.

The question of the extent of monastic learning and education in the fifth and sixth centuries in Ireland has been much discussed. It is commonly stated by Reeves and lesser writers that both Latin and Greek were taught and that classical writers in both tongues were known. All scholars agree upon the following points — that the chief subject of study was the Scriptures in Latin; that there was some acquaintance with the chief Latin Fathers; that the ability to write Latin prose was common, while the skill to compose Latin verses was only occasional; and that a few distinguished scholars like Columbanus (543–615) show a knowledge of Persius, Virgil, Ovid, Horace, and Sallust. It is almost certain, however, that there was no extended study of Greek before the ninth century. Previous to that period only an occasional rare individual was equipped to read Greek and still rarer were those who had a smattering of Hebrew.

"These monastic establishments . . . soon became great educational seminaries to which the youth of the tribe were sent not only to be trained to monastic life, but also for the purpose of receiving secular education. Each monastic church had, besides her community of monks, a body of young people who received instruction; . . . Even in the smaller monasteries the number of scholars was usually fifty. In the larger, of course, a much greater number were taught. Hence a single generation was sufficient to convert the mass of the people to be devoted adherents of the Church." [3]

The Christianizing power of these monastic communities

[3] Skene, vol. II, pp. 75 f.

has been admirably described by Skene. His words refer
particularly to Ireland but apply as well to Scotland and,
with but few modifications, to northern Europe in the period
we are considering.

"The monastic character of the Church," he says, "gave
. . . a peculiar stamp to her missionary work which caused
her to set about it in a mode well calculated to impress a
people still to a great extent under the influence of heathenism. It is difficult for us now to realize to ourselves what such
pagan life really was — its hopeless corruption, its utter
disregard of the sanctity of domestic ties, its injustice and
selfishness, its violent and bloody character; and these
characteristics would not be diminished in a people who had
been partially Christianized and had fallen back into heathenism. The monastic missionaries did not commence their
work as the earlier secular church would have done, by
arguing against their idolatry, superstition, and immorality,
and preaching a purer faith; but they opposed to it the
antagonistic characteristics and purer life of Christianity.
They asked and obtained a settlement in some small and
valueless island. There they settled down as a little Christian
colony, living under a monastic rule requiring the abandonment of all that was attractive in life. They exhibited a life
of purity, holiness, and self-denial. They exercised charity
and benevolence, and they forced the respect of the surrounding pagans to a life the motives of which they could not
comprehend, unless they resulted from principles higher than
those their pagan religion afforded them; and having won
their respect for their lives and their gratitude for their
benevolence, these monastic missionaries went among them
with the Word of God in their hands, and preached to them
the doctrines and pure morality of the Word of Life. No
wonder if kings and nations became converted to Christianity and incorporated the Church into their tribal institutions
in a manner which now excites our wonder, if not our suspi-
cion. The lives of the saints show us these missionaries,
owing to their devoted and self-denying lives, first received

with respect by some chief, then obtaining a grant of land to found their monastery, and the people soon after converted by the preaching of the Word of God." [4]

When we turn from Scotland to England to review the part played by monasticism in the conversion of the Saxon heptarchy we find the record almost equally impressive. Though the monastic system in England was an institution less completely dominating than in the Celtic lands, it provided both the leaders and the centers which made possible the Christianization of the seven kingdoms. In the words of Alfred Plummer, "It is hardly an exaggeration to say that the English nation owes its Christianity entirely to those who lived the monastic life according to the rule of Rome or the rule of Iona; and thus to the first generations of Christians among the Saxons and Angles monasticism must have seemed an essential feature in Christianity. They had no experience, and they had never heard, of Christianity apart from monasteries and monks. Consequently the monastic system had a hold upon the gratitude and affection of the people which it often lacked elsewhere. When every missionary center was a convent and every convent a missionary center, those who had learned the faith from its inmates, and were retained and strengthened in it by their help, had a reverence for an institution to which they owed so much, and took a pride in what seemed to be at once essentially Christian and national." [5]

Kent. Gregory the Great, whose influence dominated the mission of Augustine, "although not technically a monk, was a very ideal monk in his heart and aspirations . . . He idealized the monkish life and monkish standards . . . With this ideal of life, he was the first churchman of great parts who deliberately placed the monk's rôle and career above that of his secular brethren." [6] The leader of the mission to England selected by the Pope was the prior of his

[4] Skene, vol. II, pp. 73 f. [5] A. Plummer, vol. I, p. 161.
[6] Howorth, St. Augustine, pp. x f.

own monastery at Rome, and his companions (except for Frankish interpreters) were all monks — most of them lay monks. As soon as King Ethelbert had assigned them a lodging-place in Canterbury "they began to imitate the apostolic manner of life in the primitive Church; applying themselves to constant prayer, watchings, and fastings; preaching the Word of life to as many as they could; despising all worldly things, as in nowise concerning them; receiving only their necessary food from those they taught; living themselves in all respects conformably to what they taught, and being always ready to suffer any adversity . . ." [7] In other words, they at once resumed their monastic manner of life and conducted their mission with the monastery as a base, much in the style of the later friars, travelling about to preach, mostly in the open air, and holding occasional gatherings for baptism. The first of Gregory's "Responses" to Augustine strongly emphasizes the importance of maintaining the monastic life. It assumes that Augustine, though a bishop, will continue to live as a monk in community with his clergy, just as Gregory himself, when at Constantinople, had organized his household after the monastic pattern.

In consequence of the character of the mission, the organization of the Church at this time was monastic rather than parochial. For long there were few secular clergy and no parishes or parish churches. The only parishes, in fact, were the dioceses which were called *parochiae*.

Northumbria. As we have described in the previous chapter, Aidan was consecrated bishop at Iona in 635, at the request of King Oswald, and sent to Northumbria to aid that monarch in the reconversion of his kingdom. Oswald gave him the island of Lindisfarne as his see, and there he established a monastery which was to serve England for the next thirty years as a missionary center and as "a focus where some of the highest art and the best literary culture of the

---

[7] Bede, H. E., I, 26. When not otherwise indicated, translations from Bede are from Sellar's translation.

period were cherished and cultivated." So far as we know, Lindisfarne was organized after the pattern of Iona and continued the discipline and traditions of Columba's foundation. It was included in the "province" of the Abbot of Iona who was looked upon by the monks as the head of their Church. The chief difference between Lindisfarne and Iona was that the former was an episcopal see as well as a monastery. Nearly all Aidan's clergy were monks, and he himself ruled not only as bishop but as abbot. After Aidan's time, however, the bishops chose abbots to govern the monastery, though the bishops themselves were monks and subject to the abbot in matters monastic. Lindisfarne was not only founded by men from Iona but sustained in its advancing work by a steady stream of recruits, including bishops as well as laymen and priests.

In 651 Aidan was succeeded by Finan who governed the diocese till his death in 661. Then Colman, another product of Iona, became bishop; but, refusing to accept at Whitby the Catholic Easter and tonsure, he returned to Iona, taking with him all of the Irish monks at Lindisfarne and about thirty of the English. For a few months, his place was taken by Tuda, who died later in 664 — the fourth and last of the Irish bishops of Lindisfarne.

Bede pays a warm tribute to the saintly devotion of the Irish founders of Lindisfarne and their successors. "The place which they governed shows how frugal he [Colman] and his predecessors were, for there were very few houses besides the church found at their departure; indeed, no more than were barely sufficient to make civilized life possible; they had also no money, but only cattle; for if they received any money from rich persons, they immediately gave it to the poor; there being no need to gather money or provide houses for the entertainment of the great men of the world; for such never resorted to the church, except to pray and hear the Word of God. . . . For the whole care of those teachers was to serve God, not the world — to feed the soul, and not the belly.

"For this reason the religious habit was at that time held in great veneration; so that wheresoever any clerk or monk went, he was joyfully received by all men, as God's servant; and even if they chanced to meet him upon the way, they ran to him, and with bowed head, were glad to be signed with the cross by his hand, or blessed by his lips. Great attention was also paid to their exhortations; and on Sundays they flocked eagerly to the church or the monasteries, not to feed their bodies, but to hear the Word of God; and if any priest happened to come into a village, the inhabitants came together and asked of him the Word of life; for the priests and clerks went to the villages for no other reason than to preach, baptize, visit the sick, and, in a word, to take care of souls; and they were so purified from all taint of avarice, that none of them received lands and possessions for building monasteries, unless they were compelled to do so by the temporal authorities.[8]

"And so we bid farewell to that old Scotic Church of Northumbria. It could not but pass away, for it could not provide what Northumbria then needed: it had but a temporary mission, but that mission it fulfilled with a rare simplicity of purpose. It brought religion straight home to men's hearts by sheer power of love and self-sacrifice: it held up before them, in the unconscious goodness and nobleness of its representatives, the moral evidence for Christianity. It made them feel what it was to be taught and cared for, in the life spiritual, by pastors who before all things were the disciples and ministers of Christ, — whose chief and type was a St. Aidan."[9]

East Anglia. Bede's account of the conversion of East Anglia includes a description of the character and work of Fursa. In him we see an excellent example of the Irish ascetic pilgrim of the early Middle Ages, intent upon the solitary pursuit of study, discipline, and the devotional life yet — as a secondary vocation and almost by accident — playing

[8] Bede, H. E., III, 26.   [9] Bright, p. 213.

the part of a Christian missionary. Born of a noble family
in Ireland, he early entered the monastic life and eventually
became a popular preacher; but in search of peace and quiet
he left his native land as a pilgrim, accompanied by a few
brother monks, and appeared in East Anglia in the reign
of King Sigbert. After a period of active preaching, during
which he converted many, Fursa built himself a monastery
on land given him by the king. But not content even with
this form of retirement, he withdrew for a year from monastic duties to lead the life of an anchorite. About 644 the
country suffered an invasion by Penda and the pagan Mer-
cians. The resulting confusion moved Fursa to depart for
Gaul where Clovis II built a monastery for him at Lagny on
the Marne, and where, not long after, he died. In him we
see a true type of Celtic restlessness and devotion. He
"wandered, as so many of his race did, from a wish to lead
the pilgrim's life, and . . . was torn in two by the love of
mankind, driving him to active work, and by the love of
solitude, driving him to the hermit's life." [10]

Essex. The Celtic monastic system played an influential
part in the Christianization of Essex. Its bishop and chief
evangelist was Cedd, trained at Lindisfarne, and later consecrated there. During the whole period of his work in Essex
he kept in close touch with Lindisfarne and continued to
look on Finan as a kind of metropolitan. While among the
East Saxons he established two monasteries after the Scotic
system to be his missionary centers, and there lived with his
monks — "a flock of Christ's servants." For the last years
of his life he was not only bishop in Essex but also abbot
of Lastingham, a new monastery in Deira given him by
Oidilwald, to which he paid frequent visits.

Sussex. Though Wilfrid, the chief evangelist of Sussex, was
educated at Lindisfarne and that kingdom is thus indirectly
indebted to the monastic system of Iona, the South Saxons

[10] Camb. Med. Hist., vol. II, p. 524.

were converted by English clergy not at first attached to a monastery. In fact, a previous monastic mission in this region had not been a success. At an unknown date before the arrival of Wilfrid an Irishman named Dicul, together with five or six other monks, had established themselves "in a very small monastery at the place called Bosanhamm, encompassed by woods and seas . . . but none of the natives cared either to follow their course of life or hear their preaching." [11] But if this was like many another Irish mission, the monks would not greatly care, for their chief aim was to enjoy an ascetic solitude and not to baptize heathen. Whether such pilgrims, in any given case, were to be successful, would depend not so much on their intentions and method but on the strength of their personalities and the receptivity of the people around them. Fursa and Columbanus, for instance, were of the same general type as Dicul but very different from him in character and in achievement. Yet if the beginnings of Christianity in Sussex are not to be traced to a strictly monastic mission, it was not long before Wilfrid had founded a monastery at Selsey which was used thenceforth as a center for his clerical fellow-workers.

During the century in which the Saxon heptarchy was converted began the work of the Irish pilgrim ascetics and missionaries on the continent. They "were marvellous as stimulators of intellectual life and as trainers of souls. This extraordinary mixture of fervor and austerity, of independence and respect for traditions, of rusticity and a lively sensitiveness, with an imagination restrained and yet impetuous, given to eccentricities and often leading to fanciful extremes — all these traits which constitute, in their contrast, the religious temperament of the ancient Celts, exercised far and wide an irresistible charm." [12]

The most celebrated of all the Irish who came to the continent in the early Middle Ages and the great initiator of Irish monastic migration was Columban. He was the product of one of the most famous of Irish monasteries, Bangor, at a

[11] Bede, H. E., IV, 13.   [12] Gougaud, Chrétientés celtiques, p. 377.

time when it was flourishing under its founder the abbot
Comgall. It was Comgall who aided him to find twelve companions, including Gall, with whom he sailed for Brittany
in 589 or 590. After visiting King Guntram at his court
in Burgundy, Columban was given his choice of any place
in the kingdom which he might wish for a monastery and
selected Anagrates [13] in the Vosges mountains, a wild spot
where stood the ruins of an old Roman castle. There he
established himself with his twelve associates. Though the
region was remote and unsettled, it was Christian country in
a Christian land, and there was even a monastery not far
away, whose abbot Carantoc once brought food to aid Columban. Within a year or two the number of monks had so
increased that Columban found it necessary to establish a
new monastery at the nearby site of Luxovium.[14] Settling
there, "the excellent man began to build a monastery, and at
the report of this people began eagerly to stream in from all
directions to dedicate themselves to the practice of religion,
so that the very great number of monks could hardly be
accommodated in one community. The children of the
nobles from all sides strove to come thither so that despising
the spurned trappings of the world, they might win eternal
rewards. The blessed Columban, perceiving that people
were rushing in from all quarters to seek the remedies of
penance and that the walls of one monastery could with
difficulty hold so great a throng of converts . . . sought
out another place, remarkable for its bountiful supply of
water and built another monastery to which he gave the
name of Fontanas." [15] Of these three monasteries, established
between 590 and 593, Luxeuil was best situated to be the
chief center and speedily surpassed the others in fame and
influence. Columban governed all three and visited them
all frequently, like Comgall in the midst of the colonies of
Bangor; but to provide them with firm and constant guidance, he put subordinate priors in charge of each. This was

[13] The modern Annegray, Dept. of Haute-Saône.
[14] The modern Luxeuil, Dept. of Haute-Saône.
[15] Jonas, I, c. 10. Munro's translation.

the more necessary since he spent a large part of his time roaming the woods as a solitary ascetic.

In all this monastic activity Columban was not concerned with missionary work in the narrower sense of converting pagans to Christianity. No such limited purpose had brought him to the continent, and upon his arrival he had deliberately selected for his foundation a region known to be Christian. The promotion of the life of ascetic devotion among such as were ready to take the monk's vows and the development of his monasteries as centers to which the neglected laity might turn for the practice of confession and penance — these were his aims. The Rule which he laid down for his monks and which has ever since borne his name is of great importance in the history of early European monasticism but has little or no bearing on missionary history. It was probably, for the most part, a reproduction of the Rule of Bangor heightened, no doubt, in its intensity by the strenuous eagerness of Columban's own spirit. "The demands he makes on his monks are by no means new; new, however, is the energy with which these demands are carried to their highest pitch;" so that a blind and absolute obedience, enforced by penalties of extreme severity, was demanded of all. "Never was the final aim of monasticism so clear in France, never ventured in such fearless earnest." Yet the influence which Columban exerted on monasticism in the Frankish kingdom, however powerful it may have been, was not permanent. For his Rule was soon supplanted, even at Luxeuil, by that of Benedict of Nursia, partly because the Columban foundations ceased to be purely Irish in their make-up but chiefly because the Benedictine Rule was more moderate and far more highly developed in its organization. As early as 663 it had become almost universal.

Of more consequence in the study of monasteries as an agency of missionary advance is the story of the growing influence of Luxeuil and of the long array of the foundations which can trace their origin to monks trained at that center. When Columban was driven from Burgundy in 610 and went to settle at Bregenz on Lake Constance, he was accompanied by Eustasius and Gall. Eustasius, Columban's successor at Luxeuil, did much to make his monastery a missionary seminary and undertook himself to cross the Swabian Alps and begin the evangelization of the Bavarians. Gall remained in the neighborhood of Lake Constance, and from the small hermitage which he built for himself arose the great foundation which bears his name. He himself was a devout recluse rather than a true missionary, declaring, "I am filled with a burning desire to pass the days allotted to me on this earth in some retreat." Yet the assumption that the monks of St. Gall, after his time, coöperated in the conversion of the Alamanni is not improbable. Few of the other monasteries whose history connects them with Luxeuil have imposing missionary records, but notable among them is that of Corbie whose first abbot came from Luxeuil and where Anskar and his fellow-workers were trained.[16]

A century after the death of Columban Boniface entered the continental missionary field. His career as the greatest of medieval missionaries affords us the best example in history of monasticism as an agency of conversion. "The ascetic ideal," as Hauck has written, "possessed a powerful influence over him; he was not *merely* a monk, but he *was* a monk." It was inevitable, therefore, in view of his own character no less than that of the times, that his evangelistic activity should express itself in and through the monastic system. The relation of that system to his work is most easily described under two heads — his development of monasticism in Germany as a missionary agency at the front and his dependence for support upon the monasteries of "the home base," chiefly upon those of England.

When Boniface began his independent work in 721 among the mainly heathen Hessians at Amöneburg, "having gathered a congregation of God's servants, he built a cell for a monastery" — the first of his foundations in Germany and

[16] For full accounts of the radiating influence of Luxeuil and lists of the monasteries directly or indirectly sprung from it, see Hauck, vol. I, pp. 285-314; Gougaud, *L'oeuvre des Scotti*, pp. 26-28; McCarthy, pp. 224 f.

the first training-center for Hessian clergy. A similar foundation, established some four or five years later, was situated
in Thuringia where "the most holy monks were gathered
together, and a monastery was built in the place which is
called Orthorpf." The third of his monasteries was founded
some time between 724 and 735 at Fritzlar in Hesse. These
three institutions are the first examples of those cells, or
rudimentary monasteries, which Boniface was accustomed
to leave behind him as centers for the future pastoral care
of newly won Christians. They were governed in accordance
with the Benedictine rule and often grew gradually into large
establishments. Under the leadership of the Abbot Wigbert
the monastery at Fritzlar soon became the model monastery
for that section of Germany. It cared for the spiritual nurture of the surrounding regions, drew scholars from near and
far, and provided a center for agricultural development.

Boniface's keen and continued interest in his monasteries
is shown in a letter he wrote in 736 or 737 to the abbot and
other monks at Fritzlar, a very personal message which re-
veals not a little of the daily life of these small communities.[17]
"With fatherly love I beseech your dilection that because our
father Wigbert is dead you study to keep with greater care
the rule of monastic life. Let Wigbert the priest and Megingot the deacon teach you the rule, and keep the canonical
hours and the Church's course, and admonish the rest, and
be 'master' of the children and preach the word of God to
the brethren. Let Hiedde the provost admonish our slaves;
and let Hunfrith help him when necessary. Let Styrme
[Sturmi, later Abbot of Fulda] be in the kitchen, and Bern-
hard be the workman and build our little dwellings when
needed. About everything necessary ask Tatwin the abbot,
and whatever he advises, do. And let each study according to
his power both to keep his own life in chastity, and in the
common life to help his companions, and in brotherly love
to abide until our return by God's will . . ."

Later notable foundations which can trace their origin to

17 Epistle 40. Browne's translation, p. 73.

the missionary zeal of Boniface are the nunneries at Tauber-bischofsheim, Kitzingen, and Ochsenfurt — all near the Main river. Under the leadership of the famous Lioba, Tauberbischofsheim prospered greatly, producing the leaders for other nunneries; and in later years the nuns from Lioba's convent were to be found widely scattered in nearly every region between the Rhine and the borders of the Slavic peoples. In 741 Boniface established Willibald as abbot of a new monastery at Eichstätt in Bavaria, near the borders of the heathen Wends. Willibald's brother Wynnebald joined him and began a little settlement in the Sualafeld between the Altmühl and the Wörnitz, which soon (c. 751) grew into the double monastery of Heidenheim, a widely known foundation combining, in separate quarters, both monks and nuns.

But the most famous of all the monasteries which owe their origin to Boniface was that at Fulda. Its foundation is described in Eigil's *Vita Sturmi* and more briefly in a letter from Boniface to Pope Zacharias. From the former source, which is full of interesting local details, we learn that Sturmi, a young Bavarian, trained under Wigbert at Fritzlar, was sent out by Boniface into the forests of central Germany to find an ideal place for a monastery. After much adventurous reconnoitering, Sturmi returned to report his selection of a suitable location. When Boniface had secured a grant of the land from Karlmann and several neighboring proprietors, he despatched Sturmi and seven other monks to set about clearing the forest, a task which they began on March 12, 744. A few months later Boniface directed the building of a stone church and a little hermitage for himself to which he was fond of retiring. In 746 Sturmi was sent for further training to Monte Cassino and thence returned to develop Fulda according to the strictest Benedictine model. By the time of his death there were at least four hundred monks in his cloister.

Meantime, in 751, Boniface wrote to Pope Zacharias describing the new monastery and dwelling particularly upon its strategic location as a missionary center. "There is a woodland spot," he says,[18] "in a wild region, remote and extensive, in the midst of the nations to whom we have preached. Here we have built a monastery and appointed monks to live under the rule of the holy father Benedict, men of strict abstinence, without wine or mead or flesh, without servants, content with the labor of their own hands. This spot I have with lawful labor acquired by means of men religious and God-fearing, especially Karlmann, formerly prince of the Franks, and have dedicated it in honor of the Holy Saviour. In this place I propose, with the consent of your piety, to restore my body wearied with old age by resting for a short time or for a few days, and after death to lie. For four peoples [Hessians, Thuringians, Bavarians, and Saxons] to whom by the grace of God we have spoken the word of Christ are severally known to dwell around this place, to whom so long as I live and have my faculties I can with your intercession be useful."

All these monasteries, of which Fulda was the most notable example, were the primary agencies in the cause of missionary evangelism. They made it possible for the mission centers of Boniface to be economically self-supporting. The generosity of nobles usually supplied the land and sometimes the buildings; and the labor of monks, according to the Benedictine Rule, developed agriculture and cattle-raising and supplied the monastic community with food, clothing, and tools. They were thus local "home bases" upon which missionaries could depend for material support. They were likewise indispensable in discovering and training native leaders like Megingot and Sturmi and scores of lesser builders and evangelists who devoted themselves, in company with their Anglo-Saxon brethren, to the Christianizing of central Germany.

In a wider sense, moreover, they were rich sources of the spread of culture. For they were not only the nurseries and bases of supply for the missionaries themselves, they served the surrounding areas as ecclesiastical, educational, agri-

[18] Epistle 86. Browne's translation, pp. 148 f.

cultural, and industrial centers. In the monastic church or chapel the gospel was preached and the sacraments administered. The monastic *schola interior* trained the rising generation of monks and nuns, while the *schola exterior* of the larger units educated children of neighboring nobles and freemen. The economic power of the people was likewise enriched by the activities of the monks. Uncultivated land was developed, improved methods of agriculture introduced, and arts and handicraft advanced in skill.

But Boniface's development of monasticism in Germany as a missionary agency in the field depended in great measure upon the support accorded him by the monasteries of England, his chief "home base." For workers, for gifts, and for prayers, he turned with confidence — and seldom in vain — to the men and women of his own Church; and most of these men and women were monks and nuns.

An excellent example of the initiation of a missionary expedition in that period is afforded by the story of Boniface's first visit to Frisia. When he had succeeded in persuading Abbot Winbert and others of the community at Nhutscelle that he was fully determined to undertake his foreign mission to Frisia, "they willingly provided for the expenses and comforts that are necessary to human life," and liberally supplied him "with the goods of this world." And when he set forth he was "accompanied by two or three of the brethren."[19] That particular enterprise ended in failure, but not because of its typically monastic character.

From the time that Boniface assumed leadership of the mission in Hesse and Thuringia (721) down to the day of his death he remained in close touch with his friends in the leading monasteries of England. His letters to English friends fill a small volume; and in the conduct of that correspondence he kept many messengers busy travelling between Germany and England.

The chief debt of Boniface to the English Church was for the courageous men and women who came out at his invita-

[19] Willibald, c. 4.

tion to serve under him. Willibald did not exaggerate when he wrote, "From the parts of Britain an exceedingly great multitude of the congregation of the servants of God had come unto him: readers, and writers also, and men learned in other arts. Of these a very great number put themselves under the instruction of his rule, and in very many places summoned the people from the profane error of heathenism. And some in the province of the Hessians, and others in Thuringia, widely dispersed among the people, preached the word of God to the country districts and villages."[20] Popes and Frankish rulers might give him letters, but it was England's monasteries and nunneries that supplied the missionaries. And thanks to the high standing and reputation of Boniface in his native land before he departed for the continent, he was able to call upon aid from home with confidence and success.

Foremost among the Anglo-Saxon helpers were Wigbert, once a monk at Nhutscelle and later abbot of Ohrdruf and of Fritzlar; Witta, the first bishop of Buraburg; Eoba, several times a messenger of Boniface and later martyred with him in Frisia; and Wiehtberht of Glastonbury who wrote home that "Boniface, our archbishop, when he heard of our arrival, himself deigned to come far to meet us, and to receive us with great kindnesses" and that "the life here is in every respect dangerous and hard, from hunger and thirst and cold, and the attacks of the heathen."[21]

"No missionary before Boniface," writes Kylie, "had ever called women to his aid." Whether or not this statement is strictly correct, at least it is true that none before Boniface had ever called such admirably effective women to positions of leadership. From Thanet and Wimbourne came Lioba, a relative of Boniface, who had already been in correspondence with him and who later became abbess of Tauberbischofsheim. Thecla, a relative of Lioba's and abbess at Ochsenfurt, Cynehild, and Chunitrud were other Saxon missionaries who may well have come at the same time.

[20] Willibald, c. 6. Robinson's translation.   [21] Epistle 101. Kylie's translation

In addition to these fellow-workers and many others of their kind who came directly from England there were still others of Anglo-Saxon birth and training whom Boniface found in Rome and elsewhere and persuaded to join his company of helpers. Famous among these were the brothers Willibald and Wynnebald, cousins of Boniface. One of the reasons for Boniface's long stay in Rome (737–8 or 738–9) was the need to secure new missionaries, and one of the first men he found was Wynnebald who had been trained at the monastery of Waldheim (Bishop's Waltham) in Hampshire but who had already been some twenty years on the continent. Boniface persuaded him to leave Rome and go to work in Germany. There he labored for some thirteen years in Thuringia, Bavaria, and elsewhere, before founding Heidenheim in 751. After Boniface's departure Gregory III called Willibald from Monte Cassino to follow his brother to Germany. There Boniface ordained him priest in 740 and consecrated him bishop in 741. He became abbot of the monastery at Eichstätt and later bishop of that diocese. His sister Walburga, educated in England, joined Wynnebald as abbess of the nuns at Heidenheim.

Other famous Anglo-Saxon fellow-workers were Lul, Denehard, and Burchard. They were evidently friends and are naturally grouped together, for between 739 and 741 they united in composing a letter to the Abbess Cuniburga of Wimbourne to whom they report, "By reason of the death of father and mother and other near relations, we have come to the German races. We have been received under the rule of monastic life by the venerated archbishop Boniface, and are partakers in his labors so far as our poor abilities allow." [22] Lul, who had been educated at Malmesbury and Nhutscelle, had gone on a pilgrimage to Rome and while there in 738 had been invited by Boniface to join him. Either then or after a return journey to England he accepted the call, and with Denehard and Burchard, who seem also to have been previously at Rome, began work in Germany. Lul eventually suc-

[22] Epistle 49. Browne's translation, pp. 81 f.

ceeded Boniface as Archbishop of Mainz, Denehard served in
Thuringia as a priest, and Burchard became the first bishop
of Würzburg.

"These men and women . . . were not only preachers of
Christianity; above all, they made indigenous in Germany a
higher view of life. The Christian civilization which had developed in England so prosperously they transferred to our
fatherland. When one realizes that they took the place of the
priests who conferred baptism at the mere wish of the recipi-
ent or made offerings to Wotan, any doubt whether Boniface
really rendered service to Germany seems almost inconceiv-
able."[23]

If the most direct and substantial aid which came to Boniface from the monasteries of England was afforded by the
volunteers who gave to his cause a lifetime of service in the
field, there were still other means by which those who remained in the cloisters at home might contribute to the welfare of his enterprise. They sent him gifts and they answered
his continual appeals for intercessory prayer.

From the economic point of view the gifts were trivial; but
they serve to remind us of the constant and loving interest
manifested by monks and nuns in the home land. The few
presents, it appears, that were sent at the request of Boniface
were mostly books — a commentary on St. Paul, the epistles
of St. Peter, the works of Bede, a manuscript of The Suffer-
ings of the Martyrs, and others. Books likewise figure
largely among the far greater number of unsolicited presents,
though "gifts," without further description, are often mentioned. Just what these were we can only guess from a few
examples — fifty shillings, an altar pall and some garments
from Bugga, and a silver bowl with two cloaks from Ethelbert
II of Kent. But it was Lul who received from the priest
Ingalice four knives, a silver curling iron, and a towel. In
return for these remembrances Boniface sometimes sent back
gifts from Germany, though most of those of which we have
record were donated to bishops or kings.

[23] Hauck, vol. I, p. 493.

Like all successful missionaries in all ages Boniface deeply desired the prayers of his friends at home and begged them in letter after letter to offer intercessions to God for his work. In one letter (Ep. 46) he appeals "to all the reverend bishops, venerable priests, deacons, canons, clergy, the abbots and abbesses placed over the true flock of Christ, to the monks humble and submissive before God, to the virgins consecrated and devoted to God and all the consecrated handmaidens of Christ, and in general to all God-fearing Catholics." "We beseech your parental clemency," he writes, "with most earnest entreaties, that you should deign to remember our weakness in your prayers, in order that we may be delivered from the snares of Satan, the fowler, and from malicious and evil men, and . . . we beg that with your holy prayers you should seek to obtain that our Lord and God Jesus Christ . . . may turn to the Catholic faith the hearts of the pagan Saxons. . . . Act now upon this our appeal, so that your reward in the heavenly court of the angels may shine and increase."

To individuals in a score of other letters he voiced his pleas, — "I beg thee, deign to pray for me," "make intercession for us," "we beg that we may be aided by your powerful prayers," "intercede before God for us sinners." And these friends, in their turn, were eager to ask that he and his companions should pray for them.

This mutual desire for mutual aid in prayer sometimes took the form of a "fraternity of prayer," a definite agreement between two persons to pray for each other. Many of these compacts for intercession were not with monks or nuns and the objects of prayer were not always connected with missionary work. Yet this type of fellowship, characteristic of the age, was a genuine factor in the monastic support upon which Boniface depended. In writing to Lul after Boniface's death, Archbishop Cuthbert of Canterbury spoke of "the mutual arrangement which was established by several letters and faithful messengers during the lifetime of Boniface of revered memory: that for ourselves and our associates, living

and dead, mutual appeals of prayers and masses should be offered to the living God. . . ." [24]

Boniface's first years as a missionary had been spent with
Willibrord in Frisia, another English monk who depended
upon monasteries of his own foundation as training centers
and bases of supply for his evangelistic work. The most important of these were Echternach (in Luxemburg, near
Trèves) and Utrecht. Echternach was safely located in
Frankish territory and could therefore serve as a settled
home base to which his workers in Frisia might look for support in men and money. Its endowments increased continu-
ously during his lifetime. Utrecht, on the other hand, was in
Frisia and subject at times to the vicissitudes of warfare and
of shifting political control. During the first part of Willibrord's missionary career it was an advanced post in pagan
territory, but later it served as the center of his archdiocese.
It was the chief but not the only monastery founded by him
in Frisia.

Unlike Boniface, who kept in constant touch with various
English monasteries and received from them a stream of new
recruits, Willibrord seems not to have maintained such close
relations with foundations in England or even in Ireland,
though there is evidence that certain monks went out to
Frisia to join him in later years. It may well be that he corre-
sponded extensively with friends in Ireland and received support from them, but no evidence for such intercourse sur-
vives. We should expect, however, a marked difference in
this regard between Willibrord and Boniface, for Boniface
was a noted and influential figure in the Anglo-Saxon Church
before he went to Germany, whereas Willibrord, who had
not lived in England since he was twenty years old, was relatively obscure.

Before the death of Boniface his devoted fellow-worker
Gregory was made Abbot of St. Martin's Monastery at
Utrecht and was afterward commissioned by Pippin and
Pope Stephen II to preach the gospel in Frisia. Highly gifted

[24] Epistle III. Kylie's translation.

as a teacher and trainer of leaders, he made St. Martin's a
real missionary seminary where Franks, Frisians, Saxons,
Anglo-Saxons, and even Bavarians and Swabians came to
study. Most noted among them was the Frisian leader Liudger, Gregory's biographer and the first Bishop of Münster.

Though never a professed monk, Liudger had received
monastic training not only at St. Martin's but also at York
under Alcuin and was deeply interested in the study and
promotion of the monastic system. When driven from the
region of Dokkum in Frisia by Saxon invaders under Widukind in 784, he went to Rome with his brother Hildigrim and
thence to Monte Cassino where for two and a half years he
studied the rule of St. Benedict with the definite purpose of
establishing a monastery in his own country. His plan later
bore fruit in the foundation of a monastery at Werden in the
Ruhr district. Though not in Saxony, it was close by the
border and exerted a widespread influence upon the missionary region beyond. In later years, when he had assumed
charge of the missionary work in the Münster area, he built
a monastery in that town which served as a training school
for the clergy of the diocese. For financial support, however,
he could not depend on new foundations in a new diocese.
Charlemagne therefore presented him with St. Peter's Monastery at Lotusa [25] in the district of Brabant, with all its ad-
jacent churches and villages.

Another missionary to the Saxons, Willehad, owed his
training to one of Willibrord's foundations. After being
driven from Wigmodia by the uprising of the Saxons under
Widukind in 782 and having returned from a pilgrimage to
Rome, Willehad went to the monastery of Echternach and
there spent almost two years in the careful study of scripture,
including the labor of copying all the epistles of St. Paul.
Thence he was summoned before Charlemagne at Eresburg
in Saxony to receive from him the gift of the small monastery
of Justina as a base of support and the commission to resume
his work in the region of Bremen. The monks of Justina un-

[25] Either the modern Looz or Leuze.

doubtedly furnished him with many of his missionary fellow-
workers.

By the first quarter of the ninth century, when the work
of Anskar begins, missionary zeal in Frankish monasteries
was at so low an ebb that he and his companions were regarded as freakish exceptions. Anskar was a Benedictine
monk at the monastery of Corvey [26] when he was chosen by
Louis the Pious to go with King Harald on a mission to Denmark, and a fellow-monk Autbert volunteered to accompany
him. Yet in dedicating themselves to the cause of evangelism
among the heathen they were placed distinctly on the defensive and found themselves in opposition to the traditions and
sentiments of their own community. When Anskar's purpose
was first announced at Corvey, "many began to express
astonishment at his strength of purpose and his willingness to
abandon his country and his acquaintances and the love of
the brethren with whom he had been brought up, and to visit
foreign nations and hold intercourse with unknown and bar-
barous peoples. Many also deprecated whilst some endeavored to divert him from his purpose; but the man of
God continued steadfast in his resolve." [27] In other words, it
was in spite of monastic influence rather than because of it
that Anskar was launched upon his career. And we can feel
certain, too, that the account we have quoted may be relied
upon, for it was written immediately after Anskar's death by
an intimate friend and was intended for readers in that very
monastery of Corbie of which Corvey was an offshoot.
Clearly the presumption was that only the rarest of souls
would undertake the work of foreign missions except under
the compulsion of authority, a compulsion that was never
exercised, for "at that time it seemed to [the abbot] to be
abhorrent and wrong that anyone should be compelled
against his will to live amongst pagans." The contrast between these monastic groups and those of an earlier age in
England and Ireland — not to mention later Franciscans,
Dominicans, and Jesuits — is striking.

[26] At Höxter on the Weser.   [27] Rimbert, c. 7. Robinson's translation.

Once Anskar had taken the lead, however, he received intermittent support from Corvey and especially from the mother monastery of Corbie in Picardy. Anskar's companion on his first tour to Sweden was the prior Witmar of Corbie, and Corbie later furnished monks for the missionary work which Anskar initiated at Hamburg when he assumed in 831 the care of that newly created archdiocese. With their aid he established there a monastery which included a school for boys. But though he could depend upon Corbie and Corvey for a limited number of recruits to serve in a fairly settled center, his work suffered from the reluctance of the monks at home to undertake any task more adventurous. After Gauzbert had been expelled from Sweden in 845, and his companion murdered, there followed a period of seven years when Sweden was without a priest; and at the end of that time Anskar, for lack of reinforcements from any monastery, was compelled to appoint a hermit named Ardgar who, after a brief stay, "moved by the desire to lead a solitary life as he had formerly done, departed [from Sweden] and sought again his own place."

Yet if monastic volunteers for service were few and cautious, financial and educational aid supplied by monasteries was relatively steady. Without it, indeed, Anskar's Danish and Swedish ventures would have been impossible. The monastery at Welanao (Münsterdorf, on the river Stör) which had formerly served Archbishop Ebo of Rheims as a base of support for his first missionary attempt in Denmark (823), was assigned for the same use to Bishop Gauzbert during the time of his leadership in Sweden (c. 832–845). And the missionary archdiocese of Hamburg looked for similar aid to the monastery of Turholt in Flanders, which supplied funds for Anskar's work and served as a training-school for Danish boys. Indeed, so dependent was Hamburg upon help from these settled bases that when Turholt in 840 passed out of the control of Louis into that of Charles the Bald and was thereby lost to the missionary cause, Anskar was gravely hampered for lack of resources and "worried by many needs and distresses." In fact most of the monks at Hamburg returned to Corbie and left him to struggle on in poverty.

What friendly interchange of gifts and correspondence may have taken place between Anskar and his friends in the home monasteries (of the sort that brought constant cheer to Boniface) we have not the evidence to determine. But we know that the monks of Corbie and Corvey were accustomed to send him books; and we have several interesting letters from the famous abbot of Fulda, Hrabanus Maurus, written to Gauzbert and his companions in Sweden. The abbot exhorts them to persevere in their evangelization and sends them various presents — a sacramentary, a lectionary, a psalter, and the Acts of the Apostles, together with vestments, altar linen, and clocks.[28]

Compared with larger enterprises in ages of greater missionary enthusiasm, Anskar's northern ventures, then, were meagerly supported. Indeed, "this lack of zeal for the mission to the pagans in the Frankish Church of the ninth century will explain in part the rapid abandonment of the missions in Denmark and Sweden after the death of Anskar in 865."[29] The situation is well described in a recent work of Berlière who writes, "When the missionaries arrived in Germany to carry thither the Christian faith, there was in Anglo-Saxon monasticism a powerful current of missionary enthusiasm, and the ranks of apostles had at their head an organizer of the first rank — St. Boniface. [But] when Anskar was preparing to conquer the countries of the North, these countries were troubled by the devastations and piracies of the Vikings; the empire was too feeble to support them; the Frankish Church was already too intimately bound to the state and too subservient to it; German monasticism was under the influence of Frankish monasticism enfeebled as it was by the continual intervention of the state in the conferring of abbatial benefices . . . its very existence threatened by

[28] *M. G. H. Epistolae*, vol. V, pp. 522 f.
[29] Moreau, *St. Anscbaire*, p. 25.

Norman incursions which paralyzed its normal life for more than half a century." [30]

Whatever part a few monks may have played in the first feeble beginnings of Christianity in Scandinavia, monasticism was not introduced into Denmark, Norway, or Sweden until after the process of conversion was formally complete. In other words, monasteries were not there the pioneer agencies of evangelism but rather the crown of a finished work.

Quite as insignificant is the record of monasticism in the conversion of Pomerania. Bishop Otto of Bamburg, "the Apostle to Pomerania," was a liberal patron of monasteries in his own diocese, where he not only built up the famous Michelberg but was responsible for establishing or renewing at least twenty-one others. Yet he was not the product of the monastic system; his mission was not initiated or staffed by a monastery; and there is no record of his founding any monasteries during his brief journeys as a missionary. In his period the organized church as such, using secular clergy and depending on episcopal wealth, was equal to the task of church extension.

The "conversion" of the Wends was so largely due to military force and colonial expansion that monks and monasteries played no perceptible part in that long drawn out agony. But in the Christianization of the last remaining heathen portion of modern Germany — East Prussia — monastic orders became once more a factor in the expansion of the Church. The story of this final campaign in the Christianization of Europe will be told in the next chapter, for its most significant feature is the effective leadership of the papacy. Here, however, we may note in advance that the earliest missions to the Prussians were initiated by Cistercian monks who were particularly active and numerous in that difficult field during the second decade of the thirteenth century. And throughout the later crusades of the Teutonic Order the newly organized Dominicans — and to a lesser extent the Franciscans — were zealous fellow-workers with the knights.

[30] Berlière, pp. 76 f.

From a general review of the share of monasticism in the conversion of northern Europe certain broad conclusions are fairly clear. The strength or weakness of monastic influence in different epochs appears, as we might expect, to depend on two factors — the vitality of monastic life and spirit and the opportunities for initiative and unhindered activity. When both are present the results are abundant; when either is absent the results are meager. During all or part of the sixth, seventh, and eighth centuries in Scotland, England, and portions of Germany and the Low Countries monasticism was a live force full of spiritual power and missionary zeal. At the same time the openings for work were numerous and the attitude of Christian monarchs usually coöperative and beneficent. Everywhere monks were not only ready but free to take the initiative and to follow their own methods. Thus the period beginning with Columba and lasting until Charlemagne is the epoch when monks and monasteries play a leading part in missionary history.

During the next three centuries, however, except for the Cluniac revival, which seems to have had little missionary significance, monasticism declined in religious vitality and in evangelistic fervor. It was just in this era, too, that the leadership of rulers and their armies in missionary expansion is most pronounced — the era when the Saxons, the Wends, and the Scandinavians were more or less strenuously converted under political, and sometimes military auspices. Even had monks been as eager for service as in earlier times, they would have received a doubtful welcome and would surely have been denied the kind of freedom they required. Charlemagne, it is true, made some use of them; but for him they were only pawns in a larger game. And in other areas than Saxony their contributions were even more clearly negligible.

It is not until the rise of the Cistercians and later of the Dominicans and Franciscans that missionary enthusiasm once more returned to revive monastic missions. And with that renewal there coincided the rise to power of the papacy as a missionary factor. But the papacy knew — as Christian kings seldom knew — how to use the monastic forces. And so it was that once more vitality and opportunity were united. Yet the time for further conquests in Europe was almost at an end. Only in East Prussia — and there only with the coöperation of the violent Teutonic Order — could monks under papal control play out the last act.

CHAPTER IV

THE INFLUENCE OF THE PAPACY

THE influence of rulers upon the expansion of European Christianity we have found to be continuous. Missionary history abounds in illustrations of it from the sixth to the thirteenth century. Monasticism, too, at least in the early Middle Ages, remains a pervasive force in the process of conversion. But the power of the medieval papacy as a factor in missionary activity is less steadily conspicuous and more intermittent and occasional in its effect. In other words, the aid of kings and princes, in view of the political organization of the time, was indispensable; the work of monks, in view of the ecclesiastical organization, was quite as plainly inevitable; but the assistance of Popes, while normally an advantage, was seldom a prime necessity. Not until the rise of the Mendicant Orders at the close of the period we are considering, did the papacy have a fit instrument ready at its command; and not until 1622, when the *Congregatio de propaganda fide* was established at Rome, was there a central missionary organ responsive to direct papal control. During the greater part of the Middle Ages, then, the work of Christianization might or might not be indebted to papal coöperation. In Scotland and Scandinavia, for instance, the whole process was completed quite independently of Rome. In most of the remaining areas missionary progress was furthered and fortified, though seldom initiated, by the papal power. Only in exceptional cases does the papacy stand out as a dominant factor.

Since we are chiefly interested in what the papacy achieved when its authority was strongly enlisted, we may well confine our attention mainly to three shining examples — Gregory's mission to England, the relations of Boniface with Rome, and the share of Innocent III and his successors in the conversion of the Prussians.

There can, indeed, be found no clearer illustration of papal influence upon missionary advance than the mission of St. Augustine to Kent. In this notable case Pope Gregory I conceived the plan, appointed the workers from his own monastery, launched them on their journey, and subsequently kept in close touch with their activities and supplied their leader with specific instructions. Furthermore, "it was a new experiment which the Pope was making. This was the first missionary enterprise on a concerted plan, sent out by the head of the Western Church to evangelize a nation." [1]

Gregory's motive was primarily religious, for even if we reject the legend of his encounter with the Anglian slave boys at Rome, we have other evidence that he knew the Angles were pagans, that he felt deeply concerned for their spiritual welfare, and that he desired to Christianize and train the few representatives of that race whom he could immediately reach. But in emphasizing the religious purpose that impelled the Pope we do not ignore the fact that he was a strong statesman active in furthering the power of the Church in Italy, in Spain, and in Gaul, and that "the invasion of England was in a very true sense the reclaiming for the world-power which was to replace the Empire, of the province which had been lost under Honorius" and a sign of the Pope's determination to bring new rulers under the sway of Rome. But, as Oman points out, "apostolic zeal is none the less real though it be combined with statesmanship, as it was in this case." And the essential motive of Gregory — and hence of the mission of Augustine — was the true missionary motive of zeal for the conversion of those who walked in darkness.

Having determined to send a mission to England, Gregory chose for the head of the mission Augustine, who was prior of Gregory's own monastery — St. Andrew's at Rome. As his companions he appointed other monks, presumably from the same monastery. The number of these subordinates we have no means of knowing. Gregory never mentions the number,

[1] Howorth, St. Augustine, p. 27.

though Bede, in relating their landing in England, says "nearly forty." But Gregory, as we learn from his letter to the Frankish kings, had charged the missionaries "to take with them some presbyters from the neighboring parts, with whom they may be able to ascertain the disposition of the Angles, and . . . to aid their wishes by their admonition." Thanks to Gregory's ignorance of England and of conditions there, the instructions he imparted to Augustine were somewhat sketchy. Judging from the records, the Pope at first simply told him to go to England and convert the Angles, and apparently arranged with him that when the progress of the mission should justify the step, he should be consecrated bishop. Probably in the spring of 596 the mission left Rome. But at Aix or Arles they halted in despair; and Augustine was obliged to return to Rome to beg the Pope on behalf of his companions, if not on his own, that the mission be countermanded. "The Pope, in reply," says Bede, "sent them a letter of exhortation, persuading them to set forth to the work of the Divine Word, and rely on the help of God." This letter of Gregory is dated July 23, 596, and thus gives us the approximate date on which Augustine left Rome for the second time, to rejoin his companions and resume his northward journey. On this occasion the Pope took several further steps to insure the success of his mission. As the letter itself tells us, he appointed Augustine abbot of the monastic group that accompanied him and thereby enlarged and emphasized his authority. It was probably at this time, too, in view of the bewildered fear of the missionaries, that he gave orders for enlisting Frankish interpreters and guides. Most important of all, he provided Augustine with commendatory letters to rulers and bishops in Gaul.

Once the Pope had despatched Augustine for the second time he could do no more than await results. How these results came about we have described in an earlier chapter. We may quote here, however, Gregory's version of the events and note his enthusiasm and continued interest. In June or July, 598, he wrote to Eulogius, Bishop of Alexandria: [2] ". . . While the nation of the Angles, placed in a corner of the world [Gregory here enjoys a little punning with *Anglorum* and *angulo*, which suggests the puns attributed to him in the slave boy story], remained up to this time misbelieving in the worship of stocks and stones, I determined, through the aid of your prayers for me, to send to it . . . a monk of my monastery for the purpose of preaching. And he, having with my leave been made bishop by the bishops of Germany, proceeded, with their aid also, to the end of the world, to the aforesaid nation; and already letters have reached us telling us of his safety and his work; to the effect that he and those who have been sent with him are resplendent with such great miracles in the said nation that they seem to imitate the prowess of the apostles in the signs which they display. Moreover, at the solemnity of the Lord's Nativity which occurred in this first indiction [i.e., last Christmas], more than ten thousand Angles are reported to have been baptized by the same our brother and fellow-bishop."

Augustine was consecrated bishop before the end of 597, but how much later the Pope received the messengers from England we cannot be certain. It was obviously before June or July 598, the date of his letter to Eulogius. Yet the communications from Gregory which respond to the good news from Augustine are dated June 601. For this long delay of three years no adequate explanation has ever been offered. But what the Pope was not doing for Augustine in 599 and 600 may be overlooked in view of what he did do in 601. For the varied and vigorous steps which he took in that year have made history.

Having heard from Augustine that he needed more workers, Gregory appointed and despatched, in June 601, a new group of missionaries, headed by the abbot Mellitus. Once again, we do not know the total number of monks, and Mellitus is the only new name mentioned by the Pope in his commenda-

---

[2] Ewald and Hartmann, *Gregorii I Papae registrum epistolarum*, VIII, 29. This edition in the *Monumenta Germaniae historica* will be referred to as "E. and H." The translations of Gregory's letters here used are from Barmby's edition, with occasional emendations. See Bibliography.

tory letters. But Bede adds the names of Justus, Paulinus, and Rufinianus as constituting (with Mellitus) "the chief and foremost." With this party, which included Laurentius and Peter, Gregory sent letters of introduction to three of the prelates previously addressed in 596 and to eight others, together with messages to the Frankish rulers, Theoderic, Theodebert, Clothaire, and Brunhild.

In addition to the letters of introduction, the Pope entrusted Laurentius with letters to King Ethelbert and Queen Bertha of Kent, in which he opens communication for the first time with these Christian rulers. The epistle to Ethelbert is of special interest as the first letter addressed by a Pope to an English sovereign. In writing it Gregory clearly implies that Ethelbert is a baptized Christian and that he needs only to be exhorted to make his subjects Christian. With a few omissions we may here quote the Pope's words:[3] ". . . And therefore, illustrious son, keep guard with anxious mind over the grace which thou hast received from above. Make haste to extend the Christian faith among the peoples under thy sway, redouble thy upright zeal in their conversion, put down the worship of idols, overturn the edifices of their temples, build up the morals of thy subjects in great purity of life by exhorting, by terrifying, by enticing, by correcting, by showing examples of well-doing . . . and you, illustrious Sir, must now be eager to pour the knowledge of the one God, the Father, the Son, and the Holy Ghost, into the kings and peoples subject to you. . . . Moreover, you have with you our most reverend brother, Augustine the bishop, learned in monastic rule, replete with knowledge of Holy Scripture, endowed by the grace of God with good works. Listen gladly to his admonitions, follow them devoutly, keep them studiously in remembrance . . . aid his endeavors by the power which he gives you from above. . . . I have sent you some small presents, which to you will not be small, when received by you from the benediction of the blessed apostle Peter. . . ."

Another pair of letters sent in June 601 are those to Augus-

[3] E. and H., XI, 37. Bede, H. E., I, 32.

tine, one concerning his miracles and one granting him the
pallium.[4] The second letter [5] runs as follows: ". . . Since
the new Church of the Angles has been brought to the grace
of Almighty God through the bountifulness of the same Lord
and thy labors, we grant to thee the use of the pallium
therein for the solemnization of mass only, so that thou
mayest ordain twelve bishops in different places, to be subject to thy jurisdiction, with the view of the bishop of the city
of London being always consecrated in future by his own
synod, and receiving the dignity of the pallium from this
holy Apostolic See which by God's appointment I serve.
Further, to the city of York we desire thee to send a bishop
whom thou mayest judge fit to be ordained; so that, if this
same city, with the neighboring places, should receive the
word of God, he also may ordain twelve bishops and enjoy
the dignity of a metropolitan. For to him also, if life is
spared us, we propose, with the Lord's favor, to send a pallium; but we wish him to be subject to your control, brother.
After thy death, however, let him be over the bishops whom
he shall have ordained, so as to be in no wise subject to the
jurisdiction of the Bishop of London. Further, between the
bishops of London and York in the future let there be this
distinction of dignity, that he be accounted first who has
been first ordained; and let them arrange harmoniously by
common counsel and combined action whatever is to be done
out of zeal for Christ. Let them be of one mind in what is
right and accomplish what they are minded to do without
disagreement with each other. But you, my brother, by appointment of our Lord God Jesus Christ, are to have authority not only over those bishops whom thou shalt ordain and
over those ordained by the Bishop of York, but also over all
the clergy [*sacerdotes*] of Britain, to the end that they may
learn the form of right belief and good living from the tongue

---

[4] The *pallium* at this time was ordinarily presented by Popes to metropolitans,
and, while not necessary (as in later days) to their exercise of metropolitan jurisdiction, it implied the conveyance of a certain authority, especially the power to establish new bishoprics.

[5] E. and H., XI, 39. Bede, H. E., I, 29.

and the life of thy Holiness, and performing their duty in faith and morals, may attain, when the Lord pleases, to the kingdom of heaven. God keep thee safe, most reverend brother."

No better example could be offered of the extent to which Gregory kept his hand on every detail of policy in the progress of the English Church and assumed responsibility for directing its expanding organization. Considering the Pope's ignorance of the Britain of his day, his plan shows remarkable wisdom and foresight. It is quite true that in large part it was impracticable at the time: England was not being converted at one sweep. Indeed, it was to be nearly twenty-four years before York had an archbishop and nearly nine centuries before the Church of England had as many as twenty-four dioceses. Augustine founded only three bishoprics — Canterbury, Rochester, and London; and it was so long before London could be regarded as Christian that Canterbury retained the primacy. Then, too, we must confess that committing to Augustine all the clergy in Britain to be taught and corrected was rather a large order. But, as Barmby well notes,[6] "It is interesting to observe that the scheme in its main features — that of two independent metropolitans, in the North and in the South, each with his suffragan bishops under him — was after all eventually realized, and that the present constitution of the English Church may be traced to this letter; only that Canterbury never yielded its primitive dignity, as had been proposed, to London."

With these epistles went a long document containing replies to various questions asked of the Pope by Augustine — a notable instance of the latter's dependence upon Gregory and of Gregory's skill in meeting the difficulties of his distant subordinates.[7] The first topic in these "Responses" we have dealt with already in considering the monastic character of the mission. The seventh treats of Augustine's relations with the British clergy. The third, fourth, eighth, and ninth sub-

[6] Barmby, vol. XIII, p. 81, n. 4.   [7] E. and H., XI, 56a. Bede, H. E., I, 27.

jects are of no missionary significance. Only the three remaining are suggestive for our purpose. Of these, one is concerned with a liturgical problem which Gregory solves in a
liberal spirit of readiness to adapt tradition to the exigencies
of the missionary situation. Another raises a question dealing with the laws of marriage, and Gregory's reply is an early
example of the missionary principle that obligations incurred
before baptism, even though contrary to Christian morality,
have a claim to be respected. Still another difficulty — in
regard to the number of bishops required for a consecration
— finds Gregory prepared to sanction unusual practices in
view of special circumstances in the mission field.

One more letter from Gregory, addressed to Mellitus,[8] was
forwarded after the mission had left Rome for England. It
is so important in a study of missionary method that we shall
here quote the greater part. "The aforesaid envoys having
departed, the blessed Father Gregory sent after them a letter
worthy to be recorded, wherein he plainly shows how carefully
he watched over the salvation of our country. The letter
was as follows: 'To his most beloved son, the Abbot Mellitus;
Gregory, the servant of the servants of God. We have been
much concerned, since the departure of our people that are
with you, because we have received no account of the success
of your journey. Howbeit, when Almighty God has led you
to the most reverend Bishop Augustine, our brother, tell
him, what I have long been considering in my own mind concerning the matter of the English people; to wit, that the
temples of the idols in that nation ought not to be destroyed;
but let the idols that are in them be destroyed; let water be
consecrated and sprinkled in the said temples, let altars be
erected, and relics placed there. For if those temples are well
built, it is requisite that they be converted from the worship
of devils to the service of the true God; that the nation, seeing
that their temples are not destroyed, may remove error from
their hearts, and knowing and adoring the true God, may the
more freely resort to the places to which they have been

[8] E. and H., XI, 56. Bede, H. E., I, 30.

accustomed. And because they are used to slaughter many oxen in sacrifice to devils, some solemnity must be given them in exchange for this, as that on the day of the dedication, or the nativities of the holy martyrs, whose relics are there deposited, they should build themselves huts of the boughs of trees about those churches which have been turned to that use from being temples, and celebrate the solemnity with religious feasting, and no more offer animals to the Devil, but kill cattle and glorify God in their feast, and return thanks to the Giver of all things for their abundance; to the end that, whilst some outward gratifications are retained, they may the more easily consent to the inward joys. For there is no doubt that it is impossible to cut off everything at once from their rude natures; because he who endeavors to ascend to the highest place rises by degrees or steps, and not by leaps . . .'"

So clear an explanation of a policy requires little further comment. It is an extreme statement of the missionary principle of accommodation, aiming to capitalize ancient habits, to adapt the new to the old, and to make as easy and inviting as possible the transition from paganism to Christianity. It sums up a general method that, in one respect or another, has characterized Roman Catholic missions in many lands and ages.

Finally, Gregory also despatched with Laurentius and Mellitus and their company not only gifts for King Ethelbert but "all things in general that were necessary for the worship and service of the Church, to wit, sacred vessels and altar-cloths, also church furniture and vestments for the bishops and clerics, as likewise relics of the holy apostles and martyrs, besides many manuscripts." [9]

Thenceforth till his death in 604 Gregory seems to have had no further communication with Augustine. His share in the work was finished. As originator, sustainer, and guide, his contribution had been manifold.

"The active life of St. Augustine lasted only eight years.

[9] Bede, H. E., I, 29.

The main lines of that life are known; of the rest we are ignorant. . . . The rest can be summed up in a word: he was
the instrument of the papacy. His personality is effaced in
his function. The original conception, controlling and
powerful, was Rome's, so that those two great names —
Gregory and Augustine — are inseparable. The glory of the
one is lost in the radiance of the other." [10]

In 619, when Mellitus became Archbishop of Canterbury,
he and Justus of Rochester received "letters of exhortation"
from Boniface V, but these do not appear in Bede. Five
years later, in 624, when Justus had succeeded to the primacy, he received a letter from Boniface V, accompanied by
the gift of a pall and granting him permission to ordain
bishops.[11] This document is the last papal message to Kent
during the period of conversion.

After the death of Gregory the Great the Roman mission
in England was no longer actively supported by the papacy.
Except for Birinus in Wessex, we know of no further reinforcements from Rome. Papal activity, during the rest of
the missionary period, was confined to a few matters of
consecration and succession and several letters to rulers and
bishops. The only communications of missionary interest
are letters from Pope Boniface V written in 625 to King
Edwin of Northumbria and to his queen Ethelberg.[12] The
letter to Edwin, like that to Ethelberg, is written in a verbose
and involved style, and there are frequent signs of corruption
in the text we possess. The Pope informs Edwin that he has
heard of the conversion of King Eadbald of Kent and of
Edwin's Christian queen Ethelberg, and exhorts the king to
follow their example by abjuring idolatry, destroying its
images, and accepting Christianity. The Pope concludes by
stating that he is sending to Edwin a cloak and a coat with a
gold ornament. The letter to Ethelberg speaks of the Pope's
receipt of the news of Eadbald's conversion and of the
Christian character of the queen herself, and warmly urges
her to work for the conversion of her husband and his people.

[10] Brou, pp. 148 f.   [11] Bede, H. E., II, 8.   [12] Bede, H. E., II, 10, 11.

And by way of assisting her apostolic labors, the Pope despatches with his epistle a silver mirror and a gilded ivory comb.

It was fortunate for England that Rome should have initiated the conversion of the Anglo-Saxons, that the Celtic Church of Iona and Lindisfarne should have contributed so richly to the process of Christianization, and that the Roman system should have ultimately triumphed.

Augustine's landing in England "signified the return of the Romans to the land of Caesar's triumphs, the bringing back of Roman language, Roman thought, Roman culture, Roman religion, and even in some measure Roman laws, to the new home of the English peoples. It was the retort of the West to the challenge of the Northmen, the last act in the drama of Roman conquest in Britain." [13] The mission from Rome "meant something more than the conversion of the English to Christianity. . . . It meant the restoration to southern Britain of that intercourse with the Roman world which it had lost by the withdrawal of the legions and the inroads of the invaders. . . . Into this great stream of civilized life, which, acting on the new Teutonic material, has made the history of the world since then, we of the Western Isles were launched by the mission of St. Augustine." [14]

The Irish evangelists of the Celtic Church contributed to the Christian life of England the fine traditions of their monastic schools — spiritual intensity, a devout asceticism, missionary zeal, and a "rich variety of personal character and life." In the transitional period of conversion their aid was invaluable. But as permanent guides of an English Church their defects were manifest. They were saintly adventurers rather than sane builders. They were incapable of unity, order, and organization on any large scale. "A Church molded on the Celtic type could never have sufficed for the needs of England. The Irish Church was too intensely monastic, too closely bound up with the tribal divisions of its

[13] Dudden, vol. II, p. 110.   [14] Collins, pp. 53–55.

people, and too widely separated from the general area of ecclesiastical civilization." [15] "Fervor and ascetic self-sacrifice are essential virtues for those who have to build up a church, but for those who have to administer a church already solidly constituted, tact, practical wisdom, and a broad charity of spirit are also necessary. The Celtic Church put before it as its highest aim the extension of the monastic ideal, as is sufficiently shown by the fact that the great tribal monastery was the center of religious life. . . . But all mankind . . . could not be swept into monasteries. . . . As an organization for the spiritual government of a mixed community the Celtic system left much to be desired. Its influence for good was much diminished by its narrow ideal. Most of all was it noticeable that it had no effect whatever as a unifying force for the nations among which it prevailed." [16] Indeed, its form of organization served only to accentuate and perpetuate local differences.

It was therefore an immense advantage to the Church of England that the Synod of Whitby and the ensuing work of Archbishop Theodore should have brought the whole Church into communion with Catholic Christianity. Through Rome and Rome's system came not only a larger outlook, a wider knowledge of a varied world, and the background of an ancient civilization, but, above all, order, organization, and unity.

At the end of the century in which Roman Christianity was winning its way in England Willibrord in Frisia established relations with the papacy. The early influences to which Willibrord had been subject during the long period of his education were such as to instill in him a reverence for the authority of Rome as necessary to the welfare of the Church, and to encourage in him an attitude of dependence upon the papacy. Before 664, the monastery at Ripon (to which Willibrord was sent when a very small boy) had been purged of its original Irish-Scottish elements, and Wilfrid had become its abbot. In 664 (when Willibrord was only

[15] Bright, p. 210.   [16] Oman, p. 292.

seven) Wilfrid was consecrated bishop of York, but he remained for some years as abbot and his pro-Roman influence undoubtedly persisted thereafter. Since Willibrord remained at Ripon until the age of twenty, he was deeply imbued with loyalty to Rome during his most formative years. Furthermore, when he went to Ireland in 678, it was to study under the guidance of Egbert who was later (716) responsible for converting the community at Iona to the Roman rule in regard to Easter, the tonsure, and other matters. Willibrord thus "belonged alike by training and by personal choice to the side which had won the day at the Synod of Whitby."

It is not surprising, therefore, that Willibrord should have seized the earliest opportunity after reaching Frisia in 690 to present himself before the Pope. "As soon as Willibrord understood that he had license of the prince [Pippin] to preach in [Frisia], he hastened to go to Rome where Sergius at that time was over the see apostolic, that with his license and benediction he might set upon the work of preaching the Gospel to the heathen, which he had long desired. . . . When his desire was accomplished, he returned to preach." [17] This first journey to Rome, as Hauck has pointed out, was highly significant. It marked the beginning of a close tie between the German Church and the papacy. For Willibrord was not merely eager, like many others, to obtain the papal blessing upon his work and to acquire relics for his churches. He definitely sought of Sergius permission for his undertaking, since he considered him the leader of the Universal Church — a conviction as to the range of papal power which was not at that time shared by the Frankish Church.

This bond with the papacy was made all the stronger when, some four years later, Willibrord acceded to the urgent requests of Pippin that he go to Rome to receive consecration as bishop at the hands of the Pope. Pippin's aim, as stated by Alcuin, was that Willibrord, "after receiving the apostolic blessing and commission," might be "fortified with

[17] Bede, H. E., V, 11. King's translation.

greater confidence as the Pope's emissary." [18] After Willibrord had arrived in Rome in the autumn of 695, the Pope "consecrated him publicly in apostolic fashion and with great solemnity, as archbishop . . . gave him the name of Clement, invested him with his sacerdotal robes, and confirmed him with the sacred pallium of his office . . ." And Willibrord then "returned with enhanced confidence" to Pippin.[19]

In view of the characteristic dependence of the Anglo-Saxon Church upon Rome it was quite natural that Boniface, setting forth from England for his life's work upon the continent, should seek Rome as his first goal. His motive was not only that of the pilgrim eager to visit the Holy City but that of the missionary, true to the Christian tradition of his race, determined to evangelize and to organize under the guidance and protection of the Pope. From the day he first entered Rome until the hour of his death as a martyr in Frisia thirty-five years later, Boniface was a consistent and devoted servant of the Holy See, in the closest relations with four successive Popes and acting always in conformity with their will and purpose.

Toward the close of the year 718 Boniface arrived in Rome and presented his credentials to Gregory II. After prolonged conference with Boniface during many months, the Pope provided him with a letter, dated May 15, 719, which commended him for his dependence upon the Holy See, authorized him to preach to the heathen, and asked him to send word of his future progress. Though no mention was made of any particular area of work, it is likely that there was a mutual agreement that the field was to be the central and southern regions east of the Rhine.

In the course of the next three and a half years Boniface labored first in Frisia and then in Hesse and Thuringia. After a period of about two years in Frisia with Willibrord, he declined the latter's urgent call to succeed him as archbishop, on the ground that he had voluntarily attached him-

---

[18] Alcuin, c. 6. Bede, H. E., V, 11.   [19] Alcuin, cc. 7, 8.

self to the Pope's "lordship and governance," had been commissioned by the Pope to serve the nations of Germany and
could not, without the Pope's authentic command, "undertake a rank so distinguished and sublime." In pursuit of the
Pope's directions Boniface then transferred his sphere of
work to Hesse and Thuringia. Finally, at some time before
the autumn of 722, "when he had cleansed many thousand
people from their inveterate paganism and given them
baptism, he directed to Rome a fit messenger, a faithful
bearer of his letter, Bynna by name; and . . . disclosed in
order to the venerable father, the bishop of the apostolic see,
all the things which by God's gift had been brought to pass
in him . . . and asked concerning things which pertained to
the daily need of the Church of God and the progress of the
people: that he might obtain the counsel of the apostolic
see." [20] In response to this report, indicating both Boniface's
success and his continued fidelity, the Pope summoned him
to Rome, examined and instructed him in matters of faith,
and on November 30, 722, consecrated him bishop.

At the time of his consecration Gregory II "gave to
[Boniface] and to all subject to him the friendship [*famil-
iaritatem*] of the holy Apostolic See thenceforth forever." [20]
The granting of this special relationship was far more than a
mere gesture of good-will. It was a definite privilege that
can be technically described and that was renewed by at
least two later Popes; and the position of Boniface as a
missionary bishop was fortified, through all his career, by
his possession in this proper legal form of a declaration of
special patronage granted by the papacy. Correlative with
the granting of this special patronage by the Pope was a
special oath of allegiance to the Pope which Boniface took at
the time of his consecration. [21]

At the same time the Pope supplied Boniface with four
letters. [22] The first of these is a strictly formal document addressed to the clergy and people, introducing Boniface to

[20] Willibald, c. 6. Robinson's translation.
[21] Ep. 16.   [22] Epp. 17, 18, 19, 20.

them as their bishop. A second letter, addressed to the rulers, clergy, and all Christians in Germany, is freer in style and adapted, in its contents, to the actual situation of the bishop. A third letter was inscribed to certain Thuringian nobles and to all Thuringian Christians, and a fourth to Charles Martel.

In the light of all these documents, dated at approximately the time of Boniface's consecration, we are left in no doubt as to his close relationship with the papacy. The Pope consecrated him at Rome, granted him a special form of patronage, required of him an exacting oath of allegiance, and commissioned him to assume the task of evangelizing throughout a wide area of Germany and of organizing and reforming the existing Church in those parts in dependence upon the Holy See and in accordance with the canon law of Rome. To aid him in this heavy undertaking the Pope provided him with letters of introduction which emphasized his direct attachment to the Pope, rather than to any lesser metropolitan, and which, at least indirectly, pressed the claims of the papacy to an authority in Germany and the Frankish kingdom not merely moral, as heretofore, but legal.

As to the effect of the papal will and purpose upon the life work of Boniface a paragraph of Hauck's is illuminating.

"It is plain," he writes, "that the original thoughts and purposes of Boniface gradually receded. Gregory set before him another aim than that which he had chosen for himself; he had wished to follow Christ by leaving his home and proclaiming the gospel among strangers; he had rejoiced in the thought of being a leader of willing scholars, especially in the study of holy Scripture (cf. Ep. 9). He wished at the same time to act in close communion with the Roman Church; but his bond with the Pope drew him on into that Roman political activity which aimed at a universal Church: as the champion of what Rome declared to be ecclesiastical law he was to pass beyond the Alps. Yet though his purpose of missionary activity was not given up, the missionary was to be at the same time a reformer; and it was inevitable that the activity of the latter should force that of the former into the background. When that took place, when Boniface ceased to be a missionary and became entirely an ecclesiastical organizer, the necessity was painful to him, for missionary service remained his ideal. It was granted to him in old age to offer his life in that cause. But the work of his years of maturity was chiefly concerned with another purpose. Who can find fault with this dislocation of his task? For it was far more important that a reforming influence should be exerted upon the depraved Frankish Church than that the conversion of Saxons and of the free Frisians should begin some decades earlier." This shift of emphasis that Boniface found so harassing has resulted, Hauck adds, in giving to his personality a significance that has outlasted centuries.[23]

After visiting Charles Martel in the spring of 723, Boniface resumed his labors in Hesse. Some time in the following year he sent a report of his progress to Gregory II who wrote him a reply, dated Dec. 4, 724. In a letter to the Thuringians [24] written at about the same time and evidently at the request of Boniface, the Pope reminds them of Boniface's commission as their bishop and bids them obey him, honor him, and incline their hearts to his teaching. He warns them to leave off idolatry and heathen sacrifices and to observe and do in all things what Boniface teaches. Finally he commands that they build their bishop a house and construct churches for themselves. It was probably in the spring of 725, after this epistle had been written and received, that Boniface went to work in Thuringia.

The next letter which Gregory II wrote to Boniface, dated November 22, 726,[25] was in answer to a letter from Boniface sent by the messenger Denual and containing not only a favorable report of his labors but also many questions of a practical kind to which he sought answers from the Pope. The problems raised were concerned with marriage and the marriage relation, with the disciplining of vicious priests,

---

[23] Hauck, vol. I, pp. 464 f.   [24] Ep. 25.   [25] Ep. 26.

with the administration of the sacraments, and with other questions not of missionary significance.

When Gregory II died in February 731 and Gregory III succeeded him, "again the saint's messengers came to Rome and addressed the holy bishop of the Apostolic See, and showed to him the former alliance of friendship which his predecessor mercifully conferred upon St. Boniface and his household. But also they assured him of the saint's devoted and humble submission to the Apostolic See for the future; and, in accordance with their instructions, they prayed that thenceforth he might in devout submission share in the brotherhood and communion of the sacred bishop and of the whole Apostolic See. Then straightway the holy Pope of the Apostolic See offered a conciliatory reply, and granted communion of brotherhood and friendship with himself and the Apostolic See to St. Boniface and to those subject to him. And he gave the ambassadors an archbishop's pall, and sent them home honorably with gifts and divers relics of saints. The messengers on their arrival recited to Boniface the voluntary replies of the man apostolic. He now rejoiced greatly, and, being exceedingly strengthened by the devoted support of the Apostolic See, and inspired by the aid of the divine mercy, built two churches to the Lord." [26]

Pope Gregory III's reply, granting Boniface the pall of an archbishop, was written in 732.[27] In this epistle the Pope urges him "to ordain bishops, but only after pious consideration, that the dignity of bishop be not lowered." He then adds further restrictions in regard to the creation of bishoprics, limitations appropriate to an earlier day in Mediterranean lands but serving no purpose in Germany except to retard the execution of Boniface's ripening plans. These instructions remind us of the fact that when Popes gave specific directions in such matters to Augustine or Boniface their advice was generally the outcome of ignorance of local conditions and often did more harm than good. As lending power and prestige and protection, the Popes were useful to these

[26] Willibald, c. 6. Robinson's translation.   [27] Ep. 28.

missionaries; but when they were too exact in their commands and attempted to prescribe details, their instructions were sometimes impossible of execution and even injurious to the cause.

After five years of work as archbishop in Thuringia and Bavaria, Boniface went to Rome for his third and last visit in 737, "that he might enjoy," as Willibald says, "the salutary conversation of the apostolic Father." The number and importance of the problems which he was anxious to submit to the Pope may be judged from the fact that he stayed for nearly a year.

One of the points to be discussed was probably raised by the strong desire of Boniface to give up his work of church organization in Hesse and Thuringia and to devote himself to some more directly missionary task. It is altogether probable that the field of service which he sought was among the Saxons, for during his stay in Rome he wrote a letter to the clergy and Christian people of England urging them to pray for the conversion of the pagan Saxons, their continental kinsmen, and adding that for this request he had obtained the consent and approval and benediction of two Roman pontiffs [Gregory II and Gregory III]. But while the Pope was thus ready to approve the plan in general, he was evidently not willing to allow Boniface to drop his work in Hesse and Thuringia in order to lead the evangelization of the Saxons. This point is made clear by a letter from Boniface to certain of his friends in Germany in which he reported from Rome how cordially the Pope had received him and informed them that the Pope had ordered him to return to them and to persist in his former field of labor.[28]

Before Boniface left Rome for the last time in 738 (or 739) he received from Gregory III, for use in his work, three letters of commendation. One of these was addressed to bishops, priests, and abbots, of all provinces, and contains these words: "To him may the love and reverence and religion of you all deign to give assistance. . . . And if by any chance

[28] Ep. 41.

any of your ministers shall wish to join this most holy man in the ministry of exhortation of the holy Catholic faith, in no way prevent him. . . . Out of your own flock give him helpers . . ."

Another letter was addressed to the nobles and people in Hesse and Thuringia and other neighboring regions, to whom the Pope says, "You we exhort in the Lord to accept worthily from him the word of exhortation and to receive in the ministry of the Church the bishops and priests whom he shall ordain by virtue of the apostolic authority given to him. And whenever he shall find any strayings from the path of right belief or from canonical doctrine, and shall prohibit them, let him not be hindered by you in any way . . . for he who refuses obedience earns for himself damnation."

Gregory III directed a third letter to five bishops in Bavaria and Alamannia, in which he declares, "It is fitting that you should know to receive our brother and fellow bishop Boniface (now present with us) as our vicegerent, with honor worthy and due for Christ's name. From him, as appointed by us, receive and keep worthily the ecclesiastical ministry with the Catholic faith. . . . And as you shall be instructed by our said fellow bishop, so keep the Catholic and apostolic doctrine . . ." [29]

After Boniface had left Rome and had been busy for about a year in organizing the Church in Bavaria according to plans agreed upon with the Pope, the latter wrote him an epistle dated October 29, 739,[30] a message which indicates clearly how Gregory continued to direct and trust and support him. "You have told us," wrote the Pope, "of what you have done in the province of the Bavarians. Raising our hands to heaven, we give thanks to our Lord God . . ." Referring next to Boniface's organization of four dioceses, he continues, "You have done well and prudently, my brother, for you have in our place fulfilled the apostolic precept and done as we told you. . . . With regard to the Council which

[29] Epp. 42, 43, 44. Browne's translations, pp. 94–98.
[30] Ep. 45. Browne, pp. 95 ff.

you are to hold in our stead near the banks of the Danube, we instruct your brotherliness that you are there by apostolic authority. . . . Be not reluctant, most beloved brother, to undertake rough and diverse journeys, that the Christian faith may be spread far and wide by your efforts " — a superfluous warning, considering that Boniface would have been only too glad to be more of a missionary than Gregory would let him be.

After his immediate task in Bavaria had been completed Boniface returned to Hesse and Thuringia and proceeded to organize three dioceses there — Buraburg, Würzburg, and Erfurt — for which he consecrated bishops in 741. Early in the following year he wrote to Pope Zacharias asking for the confirmation of papal authority for these new bishoprics. The Pope replied, after some delay, in a letter dated April 1, 743, readily consenting to the confirmation requested. At the same time he despatched letters of recognition to Bishop Witta of Buraburg and Bishop Burchard of Würzburg.[31]

That the attitude of Boniface toward the papacy, however, (despite the fervor of his respectful language) was as far as possible from that of a weak and grovelling dependent is manifest from other passages in the long letter of 742. For the epistle includes a strong and courageous protest in regard to certain scandalous conditions permitted in Rome. Boniface particularly cites the riotous celebrations at the New Year season in the very neighborhood of the Church of St. Peter when processions of dancers throng the streets and heathenish shouting and blasphemous songs fill the air, while the people indulge in feasts by night and day, and women sell charms and amulets to all who will buy. "If all these things," he asserts, "are seen there by rude and unlearned men [on pilgrimage from Germany], it causes remonstrance and obstruction to our preaching and teaching here. . . . If therefore you, O Father, will put away such heathenish customs in the city of Rome, it would be a gain to you and a wonderful help to us in our church teaching." Plainly the

[31] Epp. 50, 51, 52, 53.

welfare of his own people was foremost in Boniface's mind, and not even respect for the Pope was allowed to stand in the way of the vigorous protest which the situation demanded. In his answer [32] Zacharias declares, "We judge these things to be detestable to us and to all Christians and pernicious. . . . So we hold it necessary for us to be careful to have nothing to do with these things." He states that Gregory III had abolished such abuses and that since they have broken out again, he himself has stamped them out.

Omitting certain communications between Pope Zacharias and Boniface which are chiefly concerned with the reform of the Frankish Church and are therefore not of significance for his strictly missionary work, there remain three letters that are relevant to our main subject.[33] All three were written in 751, three years before the death of Boniface, and show how his sense of dependence upon the papacy grew upon him with advancing years and extended (almost without distinction) to small matters as well as great. In one of these Boniface writes that he is sending Lul to see the Pope and convey private information to him, "so that when all which I send has been heard and considered, if anything which I have done be pleasing to you I may improve upon it, but if, as is to be feared, there be anything which is displeasing, by the precept of your holy apostolate I may deserve indulgence or perform the penance due. . . . I desire by the help of your prayers . . . to persevere in the friendship of the Roman Church and in your service among the Germanic races to whom I have been sent, and to obey your command."

The last part of this epistle, which has been lost, must have contained many requests for guidance and direction in a series of minor matters, since the Pope's answer deals at length with such problems — regulations about men and horses suffering from skin disease; whether nuns should wash each other's feet on Maundy Thursday; the proper age for ordaining priests and deacons; under what circumstances

[32] Ep. 51.
[33] Epp. 86, 87, 89. Translations by Browne, pp. 146, 150 f., 203, and by Tangl.

bacon can be eaten; and how many times the sign of the cross should be used in saying Mass. One question, however, was plainly connected with missionary policy, for in response to it Zacharias writes, "Also you have asked us if it is permissible or not to flee from the persecution of pagans. And as to this question, my brother, we give you the wholesome advice — If it can possibly be done and you find a place [for work], preach to them persistently; but if you cannot endure their persecution, then you have the Lord's command to go into another city."

The most important request, however, which Boniface presented in his letter of 751 was a petition that the Pope should take the new monastery of Fulda under his special protection. Zacharias replied that he had arranged for this, and we have the document in which the grant of this privilege is certified. According to its terms, the monastery of Fulda is taken under papal protection, its abbot is to be responsible to the Pope alone, and all bishops are forbidden to exercise any authority over it.

After the death of Zacharias in 752 Stephen II became Pope. Soon after his accession Boniface addressed a letter [34] to him requesting a renewal of the privilege of "familiaritas" and reminding Stephen that under three of his predecessors he had served the Apostolic See and had been greatly fortified and aided by the exhortation and authority of their letters. He then submits his record to the papal judgment in words like those which he had addressed to Zacharias two years earlier. "If in this my Roman legation which I have held for thirty-six years I have done anything useful for the said See, I desire to complete and increase it. But if I have done anything unskilfully or improperly in word or deed by the judgment of the Roman See, I promise voluntary and humble amendment."

The last letter of Boniface to Stephen [35] was prompted by a missionary motive and designed to further his final missionary expedition. It is significant that this final plea of Boniface to the papacy should have related to that mission

[34] Ep. 108. Browne, p. 268.   [35] Ep. 109.

to the Frisians with which his apostolic career began and with which it closed.

The attitude of Boniface toward the papacy was naturally transmitted to his fellow-workers and their immediate successors, so that Rome continued to stand behind and above the missionary work of the whole Bonifatian circle. Gregory of Utrecht, for example, visited Rome and was later commissioned as bishop in Frisia not only by Pippin but also by Pope Stephen II. Willehad, too, when driven from Saxony by Widukind's uprising in 782, went on pilgrimage to Rome where he was honorably received by Hadrian I, who "gave him encouragement and strength." But at this period, as the story of the Saxon wars will have reminded us, it was Charlemagne who was the leader of missionary expansion, and it was to him that the bishops and their clergy in pagan lands were responsible.

In the case of Anskar, in the following century, we have an instance of a new mission not initiated by the Pope but subsequently approved by his authority. In contrast, however, with the relations between the papacy and Augustine or Boniface, Anskar's tie with Rome was largely formal, affording him the prestige of a legate's status but little in the way of personal counsel and support.

The share of the papacy in the work of Otto of Bamberg, two centuries and a half later, was hardly more than nominal. For each of his two missionary expeditions to Pomerania the bishop obtained papal approval before undertaking them. In a record of the first journey his biographer Ebo relates that "inasmuch as Otto knew that everything in a house is controlled by the head of the house, he perceived that this difficult task ought not to be entered upon without the authority of the Bishop of Rome, and accordingly he sent messengers of distinction to the apostolic Father Calixtus [II] and obtained from him permission to evangelize the people of Pomerania." In like manner, before his second tour, he "sought the blessing of the apostolic lord Honorius [II]."[36]

[36] Ebo, II, 3, and III, 3. Robinson's translation.

From the examples of papal activity which we have already described it will be clear that, with the notable exception of Gregory the Great and his mission to England, the initiative in missionary expansion had never proceeded from the papacy. Rulers, bishops, and monastic leaders were everywhere the originating forces. More often than not they requested and received authority from Rome and profited by the support and advice of Popes no less than by the prestige attaching to the Holy See. But the part played by the papacy, while important and at times essential, was not creative or dominant. By the end of the twelfth century, however, after the long struggle with the Empire had ended, Rome at last claimed and exercised the privilege and power, never since relinquished, of initiating and controlling the spread of Christianity on the frontiers of heathendom. This assertion of authority begins with Alexander III (1159–1181) and culminates in the leadership of Innocent III and his successors in the conversion of Livland and Prussia. It is therefore at the very close of the period we are considering that papal missionary power reaches its highest point; and with the story of Prussia our survey reaches a natural conclusion.

Long before the Christianization of the Wends had been completed and before the conversion of Pomerania had even begun the first attempts were made to evangelize the Prussians — stubborn pagans of Letto-Lithuanian stock who lived in the marshes between the Vistula and the Niemen. Adalbert, who had been chosen Bishop of Prague in 983 and had retired to Rome six or seven years later, set out in 997, under the auspices of Duke Boleslav I of Poland, upon a mission to the Prussians. After a brief and unsuccessful career he was martyred on April 23 of that year. Twelve years later his biographer Bruno of Querfurt, engaged upon a similar mission, was murdered with his companions in March 1009. After the lapse of a century and a half (1141) another fruitless expedition, sanctioned by Pope Innocent II and under the leadership of Bishop Heinrich of Olmütz, seemed to prove the futility of work among the Prussians. Indeed,

it was not until the thirteenth century had opened that there
began the campaign which ended eighty years later in the
subjugation and formal Christianization of Prussia.

More by accident than design the Christian Church was
drawn once again into the dangerous field of Prussia. Two
monks of the Cistercian monastery of Lekno in Poland were
captured by the Prussians, and their abbot Gottfried, whose
name suggests that he was of German stock, was daring
enough to lead a small expedition into that country for the
purpose of ransoming them. He not only met with success
but discovered that the Prussian chieftains were surprisingly
receptive to the Christian gospel. Encouraged by this un-
expected opportunity for evangelization, he went to Rome
where he begged permission from Pope Innocent III to in-
augurate a mission. The Pope issued a bull on October 26,
1206, granting him authority for the enterprise and calling
upon the clergy of Poland to support him and his Cistercian
fellow-workers.[37] The following year Gottfried re-entered
his chosen field; but of what happened to him afterward we
have only the scantiest evidence. He converted two Prussian nobles and one of his companions was martyred. Within
three years, however, there appears in Prussia another Cistercian monk, named Christian. Writing in September,
1210, to the Polish Archbishop of Gnesen, the Pope places
Christian under the authority of the archbishop until such
time as the number of Prussian converts shall justify the
formation of a new bishopric.[38] Christian, however, though
maintaining this temporary connection with the Church of
Poland, did not work as its emissary but as an evangelist
directly commissioned by Innocent III. At the period when
his labors began the prospects for success in Prussia were
brighter than they had ever been before. By that time the
Prussians were enclosed by a ring of Christian peoples, a
situation which tended slowly to break down the national
religion and culture. The nobles in Prussia, like those in
Pomerania, discovered that conversion served to improve

[37] Preussisches Urkundenbuch, I, 1, no. 4.   [38] *Ibid.*, I, 1, no. 5.

their status in the eyes of their Christian neighbors, and no doubt internal political dissensions led some of them to promote their own cause by encouraging connections with the Poles. But the Polish associations of Christian were, on the whole, a handicap, for the Prussians had suffered so much from Polish attacks that they feared any sort of missionary advance under such auspices. It was only by emphasizing his direct relation to the papacy that Christian was able to make headway.

During the next few years Christian's work began to prosper, and Innocent continued to maintain a watchful protection. Leaders of the Cistercian Order had already begun to be alarmed at the number of monks who were leaving the cloister to take part in the Prussian mission; and in August, 1212, the Pope was obliged to write to them that such voluntary service was legitimate and that they must not hinder it.[39] A more serious obstacle was the interference of Polish and Pomeranian dukes who confirmed the worst fears of Christian and heathen Prussians by intruding their power into a new and promising field, imposing compulsory service on the Prussians. Here, too, the Pope was prompt to intervene in defense of what he and Christian hoped would prove to be an independent papal state. In the same month in which he wrote to the Cistercian abbots he despatched a message to the dukes of Poland and Pomerania, warning them not to abuse the newly converted Christians in Prussia and threatening them with ecclesiastical punishments at the hands of the Archbishop of Gnesen.[40]

By the summer of 1215 the number of converts had so increased that Christian journeyed to Rome where he received consecration as the first Bishop of Prussia. He was accompanied by two Prussian chieftains, Survabundo and Warpoda, who were baptized in the Holy City as representatives of their converted subjects. We learn of this event from two documents issued on February 18, 1216, by Innocent III,

---

[39] Preussisches Urkundenbuch, I, 1, no. 6.
[40] *Ibid.*, I, 1, no. 7.

confirming donations to Christian by these two nobles.[41]
It was such gifts as these which made it possible for Christian
to avoid the practice, approved in his time, of tithing the new
converts. Yet he must have been often hard pressed for
money, since one of Innocent's last acts was to write to a
Polish duke, urging him to donate a village for the support of
Christian, that the bishop might not have to tax his people.

The death of Innocent III on July 16, 1216, coincided with
the beginning of trouble in Prussia. It is evident from a
number of bulls issued by his successor Honorius III that the
means of support were failing the mission and that the pagans were severely persecuting their Christian fellow-
countrymen.[42] While the cause of this uprising is not stated,
it is more than probable that Polish and Pomeranian rulers
had renewed that exploitation of their neighbors which had
called forth a rebuke from Innocent five years earlier.
Despairing of any further prospect of peaceful conversion,
Bishop Christian decided on a military mission and called
for the aid of crusaders. The Pope granted him authority to
recruit for this campaign and issued several bulls in 1217
and 1218 encouraging those who could not carry out crusading vows in Palestine to enlist in the Prussian mission.[43]

The task of the crusaders was supposed at first to be
chiefly the protection of Christians against the heathen, and
the bishop obtained a papal order that no crusaders should
cross the boundaries of Christian areas without his permission.[44] He still hoped to build up a free state protected by
the papacy and imagined that he could control his temporary
auxiliaries and continue at the same time the normal activities of church expansion. Indeed, during this same period,
he was securing papal assistance in the enlistment of secular
missionary priests and the founding of schools. But once
having appealed to force, he became the victim of his own
policy. The Pope might warn the assembling army — as its
forces drew together from Germany, Bohemia, Poland, and

[41] *Ibid.*, I, 1, nos. 9, 10.   [42] *Ibid.*, I, 1, nos. 15, 16.
[43] *Ibid.*, I, 1, nos. 15, 16, 20, 21.   [44] *Ibid.*, I, 1, no. 16.

Pomerania — that its purpose was "to convert to the Lord, not to subjugate," but the common aim changed all too easily to that of conquest. Prolonged warfare ensued, and Kulmerland and the border districts were laid waste. Yet there was great scarcity of funds and the contest was everywhere indecisive. Instead of the expansion which he had anticipated, Bishop Christian found his clergy dwindling and his church members disappearing, and finally he himself had to leave the country. Three years later, through the generous coöperation of Duke Conrad of Masovia and the Bishop of Plock, he was restored to authority in the Christianized district of Kulmerland. There he enjoyed the status of a territorial lord, endowed with landed possessions and with half the ducal income; but his evangelistic work among the heathen was at an end. Once again he was to live among the Prussian pagans (1233–1239), but only as a prisoner. His ultimate failure is not difficult to explain. Trusting the crusaders to be disciplined and conscientious subordinates, he found them unruly and unscrupulous oppressors of Christians and pagans alike. They had little inducement to work in the interests of a foreign lord, the Pope, and of his representative the bishop. They wanted to win profit for themselves from the subjugation of Prussian territory and to treat those whom they conquered as vassals. Even papal bulls were not sufficient to make them accept the baptized Christians as free men, still less to rouse their enthusiasm for turning pagans into Christians. In consequence they did just enough damage to ruin the existing mission. But their numbers were too few and their discipline too lax to reap even the dubious rewards of the ruthless and persistent use of force.

After some years of intermittent fighting, during which the pagan Prussians maintained their military superiority, Duke Conrad of Masovia turned for help to Herman of Salza, the head of the Teutonic Order. The *Ordo fratrum domus hospitalis Sanctae Mariae Theutonicorum* in Jerusalem, commonly known as the Teutonic Order, was one of the three great military and religious Orders which sprang from the

Crusades. In 1190, during the Third Crusade, it had been founded as a hospital by certain citizens of Bremen and Lübeck, and in 1198 had been raised to the rank of an Order of Knights. Begun as a form of charity, it grew into a military club to which only Germans of noble birth could be admitted; and it finally developed into a sort of chartered corporation not unlike the British East India Company. For some fourteen years before the call to Prussia came the Order had been serving in Transylvania, then Christian territory. In summoning the Teutonic Knights to his aid, Conrad offered to their leader the territory of Kulmerland and certain border districts as a base for the conquest of Prussia, but Herman was not ready to accept the offer until he had received authority from the Emperor Frederick II. This he obtained in the form of a document from Frederick dated at Rimini in March 1226. The emperor empowered the Order to conquer and possess Prussia and granted to Herman in that territory the rights of a prince of the Empire.[45] In 1230 the Order entered Prussia to begin its campaign, and in that same year Bishop Christian signed an agreement with the knights, turning over to them all the possessions he had received from Duke Conrad and the Bishop of Plock. The balance was swinging more and more to the side of military methods and political control, and the possibility of realizing the original theory of a free papal state began to disappear. During the early period of conquest, it is true, the Pope recognized the rights of the Order only with limitations, and Christian still attempted to guard against the complete sovereignty of the knights. There were thus, for a time, two sovereignties in the land — the Pope represented by Christian and the emperor represented by the Teutonic Order. But the odds were all in favor of the Order, and when Christian was captured by the Prussians in 1233, the knights not only did nothing to rescue him but took advantage of the occasion to extend their power and even to draw the Pope toward their side.

[45] Preussisches Urkendenbuch, I, 1, no. 56.

Meanwhile, in spite of frequent resistance, the crusaders had been steadily pushing their conquests, marking their progress by the erection of great fortresses which later grew into towns — Thorn in 1231, Kulm in 1232, and Marienwerder in 1233. In 1234 the Order incorporated into its organization the Knights Brethren of Dobrin (founded in the previous decade by Conrad of Masovia) and launched a grand crusade in which it was joined by several Polish and Pomeranian princes. The result was a decisive victory which brought under control the whole of Kulmerland.

At this point Pope Gregory IX took a step which solved for the time being the question of sovereignty in Prussia. By agreement with the leaders of the Teutonic Order he received from them all the land which they had won by donation and conquest and granted it to them as a fief.[46] Three years later, in 1237, the Teutonic Order absorbed the Knights of the Sword who had been engaged in converting Livonia by force. Strengthened by this large accession to their ranks and supported by growing endowments they continued their process of conquest. By the summer of 1243 Pope Innocent IV judged the time to be ripe for the division of Prussia into four dioceses and commissioned his legate William of Modena to carry out the plan. The bishoprics were Kulm, Pomesania, Ermland, and Samland. In each division one-third of the land was to go to the bishop and two-thirds to the Order. The bishops were to receive the temporal investiture from the papal legate.[47]

After a dozen years in Prussia, ostensibly devoted to Christian work, what had the Order to show as a missionary enterprise? It is clear, for one thing, that many of the vices and defects so noticeable among the earlier crusaders from 1217 to 1230 were no less apparent among the Teutonic Knights. The newly baptized converts had been promised by Bishop Christian, acting for the Pope, as full a measure of personal freedom as they had enjoyed before conversion.

---

[46] Preussisches Urkundenbuch, I, 1, no. 108. Bull of Aug. 3, 1234.
[47] Ibid., I, 1, nos. 142, 143, 144.

This pledge, in very many cases, the Order ignored. The knights needed assistance in the form of labor, provisions, taxes, and military service and often obtained what they wanted by force. Worse than this illegal oppression of Christians was the frequent reluctance of the knights to allow the building of churches and even to admit seekers after baptism. Since the heathen could be treated more harshly than the Christians there was no economic inducement to increase the number of the baptized. The colonizing policy of the Order was here in sharp conflict with its missionary purpose.

Yet, in spite of mixed motives, the Teutonic Order was, in some respects, a positive missionary force. The priests who were attached to it served only as chaplains who cared for the knights; but the Order coöperated from the beginning with Dominican missionaries. The Cistercians had been the only order working under Bishop Christian, but with the coming of the knights in 1230 Gregory IX assigned to the Dominicans the task of preaching the new crusade. This type of preaching, however, was not missionary in the ordinary sense, for it simply meant rousing the better classes all over Germany, Bohemia, Poland, and other countries to go and fight the Prussians. Yet once the crusade had begun to succeed, many Dominicans were to be found as genuine missionaries in pagan districts. Subject only to the Pope, they could be taken into service by the Order and used for its purposes. The interests of the Christians, never wholly safe in the hands of the knights, were to some extent guarded by the papal legate William of Modena who spent four or five years at intervals between 1228 and 1242. But for the most part the converts had to look to the friars for protection, and the friars, on the whole, were inclined to be indulgent to the knights and to avoid any disciplinary measures which would disturb the favorable relations between the monastic and the military orders. "The [Teutonic] Order, therefore, did Christianizing work, but with the help of a corps of missionaries who could guarantee the knights that they would not keep too strict an eye upon them and that they understood the harsh necessities of colonial policy." [48]

In consequence of too feeble control by the representatives of the Pope, the Christian Prussians became so desperate under Teutonic oppression that they revolted in 1245 and sent representatives to plead their cause at Rome. That they were ready to lay their case before the Pope shows how widely the papacy was known to stand for their right to freedom and reminds us that the revolt was not against Christianity but against the Order. The outcome of several years of conflict and negotiation was a treaty of peace brought about by the papal legate Jacob of Lüttich and signed at Christburg on February 7, 1249.[49] Its terms included a requirement that the Order should recognize what the Pope and Bishop Christian had long since promised the Prussians — their direct subordination to the papacy and the right of freemen to retain their freedom after conversion. Furthermore, both knighthood and ordination to the priesthood were to be open to Prussians. Yet this same treaty which diminished the sovereign rights of the Order in favor of the papacy, contained a provision valuable to the Order and dangerous to the Prussians. It was expressly agreed that if the Prussians should again show themselves apostates in a new revolt (provided the Order was not guilty of causing it) they should lose their freedom. Such a clause must have offered to the Teutonic Knights the strong temptation to instigate a rebellion for which they could disavow responsibility and through which they might obtain a free hand in dealing with their privileged subjects. But to their credit it appears that for the next nine years no complaints from the Prussians are on record. During this period the mission made progress, and the military campaign against the pagan population was resumed. A successful expedition in the extreme northeast led to the founding of Memel in 1251; and three years later, with the aid of King Ottokar of Bohemia, a part of Samland was conquered and the fortress of Königsberg established.

[48] Blanke, *Entscheidungsjahre*, pp. 36 f.   [49] Preus. Urk., I, 1, no. 218.

In the year 1258, however, we begin to hear again the old accusations of injustice against converts on the part of the Order, and within two years a new rebellion broke out. The knights, of course, were able to find defenders who could assure the Pope that the Order was guiltless. No effort, therefore, was made by the papacy on behalf of the Prussian Christians who were, in effect, turned over to the will of the Teutonic Brethren. There then ensued fourteen years of fighting during which the knights made themselves masters of the whole of Prussia. The remaining pagans were compelled to receive baptism and to accept, with those already Christianized, the status of subjects who had no rights that need be respected. Within another decade, by 1283, the last pagan leader had fled from the country, and the "Christianization" of a war-torn land was complete. Meanwhile, for fifty years or more, German immigrants had been building up the fortified cities and settling as peasants in the open country. Through assimilation or extermination the Prussians had ceased to exist as an independent race. Whatever had been the avowed purpose of the Teutonic Knights, their enterprise had been a failure from the Christian point of view. Colonial exploitation and organized warfare could be carried on successfully only at the expense of genuine missionary activity. The aims of the Order were fatally at odds with one another, and the Church in Prussia paid the penalty.[50]

[50] In writing this section I have been much aided by F. Blanke's two studies, *Die Missionsmethode des Bischofs Christian von Preussen* and *Die Entscheidungsjahre der Preussenmission (1206–1274).*

CHAPTER V

THE MISSIONARY MESSAGE

FROM the point of view of the modern student one of the most interesting subjects in missionary history is the content of the Christian message at different periods. What did Christianity mean to the evangelists of this or that day? What did they preach about to their pagan audiences? What features of their religion did they emphasize and to what motives did they appeal in seeking to convert their hearers? These are questions that we naturally ask, and yet they are questions that seldom attract the attention of the early biographers to whom we must look for an answer. The saints' Lives which constitute our chief sources are largely concerned with praising the virtues and magnifying the deeds of their heroes. No motive prompts the writers to report the content of the evangelistic message; and we have therefore to depend upon meager bits of testimony disclosed almost by accident. Certain common features, however, seem characteristic of the whole medieval period.

There is small evidence, for example, as to what missionaries preached about in sixth-century Scotland. Indeed, the only extensive statement I have discovered is a sermon of Kentigern's addressed to a mixed crowd of Christians and heathen. But even if Joceline, the author of Kentigern's Life, had hints from the old Celtic Life which he used, his production can hardly be accepted as good evidence for the sixth century. At least, however, it gives us a conventional twelfth-century conception of what a missionary message ought to be, and as such it is worth quoting.

"[Kentigern] showed that idols were dumb, the vain inventions of man, fitter for the fire than for worship. He showed that the elements in which they believed as deities were creatures and formations adapted by the disposition of their Maker to the use, help, and assistance of men. But Woden, whom they, and especially the Angles, believed to be the chief deity . . . and to whom the fourth day of the week is dedicated, he asserted with probability to have been a mortal man, King of the Saxons, by faith a pagan, from whom they and many nations have their descent. His body, he continued, after many years had passed, was turned into dust, and his soul, buried in hell, endureth the eternal fire. By these and similar arguments casting forth the worship of idols from their hearts, he proved to them the Almighty God, Three and One, to be the Creator of all things from the very beauty of the visible creation; and after that, preaching to them the faith that is in Jesus Christ and the Sacraments of faith, he showed by the most true and lucid demonstrations that there is none other name under heaven, believing in which men may be saved, but only the name of our Lord Jesus Christ. . . . After being catechized, they renounced Satan and all his pomps and works, were washed in the saving laver in the name of the Holy Trinity; and so anointed with the sacred chrism and oil, and incorporated into the body of the Church, they became members of Christ." [1]

This message is typical of much other medieval missionary preaching in its attack upon the folly of idolatry and in its positive presentation of the Christian doctrines of the Creation, the Trinity, and salvation through Christ by means of the sacraments.

There are but few instances in Bede of the form which the Gospel message took when addressed to heathen, and such as there are may be supposed to represent Bede's idea of what ought to have been said rather than any exact reproduction of the speaker's words. They are valuable, however, as indicating the kind of arguments thought to be effective in the early eighth century and therefore likely to have been used in the seventh.

Paulinus is reported to have said to Edwin of Northumbria: "Behold, by the gift of God you have escaped the hands of the enemies whom you feared. Behold, you have obtained of His bounty the kingdom which you desired. . . .

[1] Jocelinus, c. 32.

Accept the faith, and keep the precepts of Him who, delivering you from temporal adversity, has raised you to the honor of a temporal kingdom; and if, from this time forward, you shall be obedient to His will, which through me He signifies to you, He will also deliver you from the everlasting torments of the wicked, and make you partaker with Him of His eternal kingdom in heaven." [2] Here we find an appeal to worldly prosperity as a sign of God's favor and the promise of reward in heaven after death, combined with a threat of punishment in hell for failure to follow God's command.

Another fragment appears in the story of the conversion of Peada of the Middle Angles where we read that "when he heard the preaching of the truth, the promise of the heavenly kingdom, and the hope of resurrection and future immortality, he declared that he would willingly become a Christian." [3] And here again we note the emphasis upon rewards in the future life.

Of King Oswy's frequent conferences with King Sigbert of Essex it is reported: "He used to endeavor to convince him that those could not be gods that had been made by the hands of men; that a stock or a stone could not be proper matter to form a god, the residue whereof was either burned in the fire, or framed into any vessels for the use of man, or else was cast out as refuse, trampled on and turned into dust. That God is rather to be understood as incomprehensible in majesty and invisible to human eyes, almighty, eternal, the Creator of heaven and earth and of mankind; who governs and will judge the world in righteousness, whose eternal abode must be believed to be in heaven, and not in base and perishable metal; and that it ought in reason to be concluded that all those who learn and do the will of Him by whom they were created, will receive from Him eternal rewards." [4] Though this passage alludes to the familiar rewards in heaven, it is primarily an example of the equally familiar attack upon the folly of idolatry and reproduces closely the thought of Isaiah 44.

[2] Bede, H. E., II, 12.   [3] Ibid., III, 21.   [4] Ibid., III, 22.

A similar approach to the pagan mind is that of Pope Boniface V in his letter to King Edwin of Northumbria. [5] The Pope refers to the rewards of "eternal life" and of baptism as bringing the hope of dwelling "in the brightness of eternal glory"; but most of his appeal consists of an argument setting forth the futility of idolatry. He quotes the words of the Psalmist — "eyes have they, but they see not, etc.," and then continues, "For how can they have power to help any man, that are made out of corruptible matter, by the hands of your inferiors and subjects, and on which, by employing human art, you have bestowed a lifeless similitude of members? which, moreover, unless they be moved by you, will not be able to walk; but, like a stone fixed in one place . . . have no power of doing harm or good. We cannot, therefore . . . conceive how you come to be so deceived as to follow and worship these gods, to whom you yourselves have given the likeness of a body. It behooves you, therefore, by taking upon you the sign of the Holy Cross, by which the human race has been redeemed, to root out of your hearts all the accursed deceitfulness of the snares of the Devil, who is ever the jealous foe of the works of the Divine Goodness, and to put forth your hands and with all your might set to work to break in pieces and destroy those which you have hitherto fashioned of wood or stone to be your gods. For the very destruction and decay of these, which never had the breath of life in them, nor could in any wise receive feeling from their makers, may plainly teach you how worthless that was which you hitherto worshipped."

The writer then appeals to the king to submit to the God who created him, "who sent His only-begotten Son for your redemption, to save you from original sin, that being delivered from the power of the Devil's perversity and wickedness, He might bestow on you a heavenly reward."

With these references in Bede we may compare a passage from Eddius's Life of Wilfrid composed in the early part of the eighth century. Wilfrid is recorded as saying to the

[5] Bede, H. E., II, 10.

South Saxons: "Repent you, for the kingdom of God is at hand, and let each one of you be baptized in the name of God the Father, and of the Son and of the Holy Ghost." Furthermore, "he elaborately described . . . the works of Almighty God to confound idolatry, from the beginning of the world down to the day of judgment, when eternal punishment will be prepared for sinners and everlasting life for the elect of God."[6] Once more we find the emphasis upon the judgment after death and the ensuing rewards and punishments.

The nearest approach to an account of the content of Willibrord's missionary message is his reply to King Radbod of Frisia when the latter rebuked him for violating the sanctuary of the god Fosite. According to Alcuin, Willibrord retorted as follows: "What you worship, O King, is not a god, but the devil, who holds you ensnared in the vilest error in order that he may deliver your soul to eternal fire. For there is no god but the One, who created heaven and earth, the sea, and all that is in them; and those who worship Him in true faith will have eternal life. As His servant I bear witness before you this day, so that you may now at last turn to wisdom from the vanity of ancient error to which your fathers adhered; that, believing in the one omnipotent God, our Lord Jesus Christ, and being baptized in the font of life, you may wash away all your sins; and that casting away all wickedness and unrighteousness, you may henceforth live as a new man in all temperance, righteousness, and holiness. If you do this you will enjoy eternal glory with God and His saints; if, however, you spurn me who now set before you the way of life, then be fully assured that, with the devil whom you obey, you will suffer everlasting punishment and the flames of hell."[7]

We note here the familiar promise of reward in heaven and the threat of punishment in hell. In addition, we may safely infer from the speaker's strong emphasis on the ethical im-

[6] Eddius Stephanus, c. 41.
[7] Alcuin, *Vita Willibrordi*, c. 11. Grieve's translation.

plications of baptism that he would not countenance compulsory baptism — a conclusion ratified by all that we know of his missionary career.

There is no surviving example, so far as I can discover, of Boniface's preaching to heathen. His letters contain many homiletical passages, but they are all addressed to Christians. The so-called "Sermons" of Boniface are not authentic. They were composed after his time and are quite different in form and content from his letters. But if we do not know how Boniface was accustomed to present the Christian message to pagans, we do know how he was advised to approach them by Bishop Daniel of Winchester. And while it appears unlikely, from what we know of Boniface and his methods, that he took Bishop Daniel's advice, this famous letter is worth quoting at length as showing the well-considered policy approved by a distinguished ecclesiastical leader of the eighth century who had direct knowledge of missionary conditions.

". . . Out of devotion and good-will," wrote the bishop, "I have sought to make to thy prudence a few suggestions that thou mayest know how best in my judgment to overcome promptly the obstinacy of ignorant minds. Thou shouldst not offer opposition to them concerning the genealogy of their false gods. Thou shouldst suffer them rather to claim that they were begotten by others through the intercourse of man and woman; then thou canst show that gods and goddesses who were born after the manner of men were men rather than gods, and in that they existed not before, had therefore a beginning.

"When they have learned perforce that the gods had a beginning, since some were born of others, they must be asked whether they think this universe had a beginning or was always in existence. If it had a beginning, who created it? For certainly they cannot find for the gods begotten before the establishment of the universe any place where these could subsist and dwell; by the universe I mean not merely the visible earth and sky, but the whole extent of space, which the heathen themselves can grasp with the imagination. But if they maintain that the universe always existed without a beginning, seek to refute and convince them by many arguments and proofs. If they go on contending, ask them: Who ruled it? How did they reduce beneath their sway and bring under their jurisdiction a universe that existed before them? Whence and by whom and when was the first god or goddess constituted or begotten? Do they suppose that the gods or goddesses still beget other gods and goddesses? If they do not, when or why have they ceased? If they do, the number of gods must now be infinite; and who is the most powerful among so many and such great beings, is unknown to mortals, so a man must be on his guard for fear of offending the strongest. Do they think the gods should be worshipped for temporal and present blessings, or for an eternal and future reward? If for a temporal, let them show in what respect the heathen are happier than the Christians. What again do the heathen mean to confer by their sacrifices upon their gods, who have all things under their sway; or why do the gods leave it in the power of those subject to them to decide what tribute to offer? If they need such things, why could they not themselves have made a better choice? If they do not need them, the people are wrong to suppose that the gods can be appeased with such offerings of victims.

"These questions, and many like them, which it would take too long to enumerate, thou shouldst propose to them in no irritating or offensive manner, but with the greatest calmness and moderation. And from time to time their superstitions should be compared with our, that is Christian, dogmas, and touched upon indirectly, so that the heathen more out of confusion than exasperation may blush for their absurd opinions, and recognize that their detestable rites and legends do not escape our notice.

"It would also be natural to infer that if their gods are omnipotent and beneficent and just, not only do they reward their worshippers, but punish those who despise them. But if they do both in the temporal order, why do they spare the Christians, who turn nearly the whole world from their worship and overthrow their statues? And these, too, that is the Christians, possess the fertile lands and the provinces fruitful in wine and olives and overflowing with other riches, and have left them, that is the heathen, with their gods, only the frozen lands in which these latter, banished from the whole world, are wrongly thought to hold sway.

"There must be constantly brought before them the supremacy of the Christian world: by comparison, those who persevere in the old-time vanity are very few.

"And that they may not boast of the sway of the gods over these people as legitimate and existing always from the beginning, point out to them that the whole world was given over to the worship of idols until, illuminated by the knowledge of the Omnipotent God, its creator and ruler, it was vivified through the grace of Christ and reconciled to God. For when among Christians the children of the faithful are baptized daily, what do they do but purify themselves singly from the uncleanness and guilt of paganism in which the whole world was once involved?"[8]

Here we note that the approach is to be tactful and gradual. There is to be no direct or violent attack, no threat of hell for unbelievers, or the like. Instead, the method of presentation is intellectual argumentation of a philosophical kind suited only to dealing with individuals or small groups of some mental capacity and therefore not appropriate to mass appeal for mass conversions. Effective use is made of the argument from the power and prosperity of Christendom. The Christian Church is to that extent identified with Roman civilization and the appeal is made to join the vast majority. Yet, except for this last point, there is something academic about the whole plan which suggests the cloistered student rather than the active evangelist; and it is to be surmised that a practical missionary in Boniface's field could hardly carry out such a program except on rare occasions.

[8] Epistle 23. Kylie's translation, with corrections.

The use of direct physical force for the purpose of conversion never occurs in the history of English Christianity, nor does it mar the record of those rulers who aided Willibrord and Boniface. For that reason there is no sign that the threat of such force entered into the preaching of these earlier medieval evangelists. But by the time we reach the period of Charlemagne the menace of military compulsion was a characteristic feature of missionary expansion and undoubtedly influenced the presentation of the Gospel to pagans.

The *Vita Lebuini* by Hucbald of St. Amand was written in the last half of the tenth century, two hundred years after the death of Lebuin (or Liafwin) and is worthless as an historical source so far as the career of its hero is concerned. But it may properly serve as a source for the ideas of its author's period. As such it provides us with an interesting example of a missionary sermon which Hucbald puts in the mouth of Lebuin. It is related that Lebuin, having suffered persecution from the Saxons near Deventer and witnessed his oratory burned to the ground and his converts massacred, determined to appeal in person to the Saxons at their annual gathering at Marklo on the Weser. Arrayed in his priestly vestments, with an uplifted cross in one hand and a copy of the Gospels in the other, he presented himself to the people as they were about to offer sacrifice to their national gods. Amazed at his courage they listened to him while he said:

"Hearken unto me, and not so much to me as to Him who speaks to you through me. I declare unto you the commands of Him whom all things serve and obey. Hearken, attend, and know that God is the creator of heaven and earth, the sea and all things that are therein. He is the one, only and true God. He made us and not we ourselves, nor is there any other beside Him. The images which ye think to be gods and which, beguiled by the devil, ye worship, are but gold or silver or brass or stone or wood . . . God, the only good and righteous Being, whose mercy and truth remain forever, moved with pity that ye should be thus seduced by the errors of demons, has charged me as His ambassador to beseech

you to lay aside your old errors, and to turn with sincere and
true faith to Him by whose goodness ye were created. In
Him you and all of us live and move and have our being. If
ye will truly acknowledge Him, and repent and be baptized,
in the name of the Father, the Son, and the Holy Ghost, and
will obediently keep His commandments, then will He pre-
serve you from all evil, and will grant you the blessings of
peace here and in the life to come the enjoyment of all good
things. But if ye despise and reject His most salutary coun-
sels and refuse to correct the error of your wicked hearts,
know that ye will suffer terrible punishment for scorning His
merciful warning. Behold I declare unto you the sentence
which has gone forth from His mouth and which cannot
change: if ye do not obey His commands, then will sudden
destruction come upon you. For the King of all the heavens
has appointed a brave, prudent, and most vigorous prince
[Charlemagne] who is not afar off, but close at hand. He,
like a most swift torrent, will burst upon you and subdue the
ferocity of your hearts and crush your stiff-necked obstinacy.
He will invade your land with a mighty host and ravage the
whole with fire and sword, desolation and destruction. As the
avenger of the wrath of that God, whom ye ever provoke, he
will slay some of you with the sword, some he will cause to
waste away in poverty and want, some he will destroy with
the misery of a perpetual captivity, and your wives and children he will scatter far and wide as slaves, and the rest of you
he will reduce to a most ignominious subjection, that in you
may be fulfilled what has long since been predicted, 'they
were made few in number and were tormented with the tribu-
lation and anguish of the wicked.'"[9]

Despite the rising anger of the assembled multitude, Lebuin succeeded in escaping, thanks to the intervention of an
aged chief. His supposed speech, whether or not he ever uttered it, is quite in the manner of the period of Charlemagne's
Saxon wars.

We have no direct knowledge of Anskar's missionary mes-

[9] *Vita Lebuini.* Translation in Robinson's Conversion of Europe, pp. 383 ff.

sage, but several accounts of the public appeals of his first
and foremost convert in Sweden — the nobleman Herigar —
indicate what the latter had been taught. Even if we prefer
to give the credit for these speeches to Anskar's follower and
biographer Rimbert, we at least have evidence of what Rimbert considered the most effective way of presenting Christianity to pagans.

We may note first that Herigar describes God to his fellow-
countrymen as more powerful than their own gods and able to
control the forces of nature for the benefit of believers. On
one occasion he proclaimed, "Let us prove by miracles who
is the more powerful, the many beings whom ye call your
gods or my one almighty Lord Jesus Christ." He then proceeded on the eve of a rainstorm, to pray that God would
shield him from the rain, while the others prayed likewise to
their gods. And rain descended heavily on all present except
Herigar and a small boy who was with him. At another time,
when Herigar was ill, he prayed to God to heal him, rejecting
the pleas of his pagan friends that he should turn to their
gods; and as a result he was entirely cured.

Again we find Herigar, on a critical occasion, urging upon
the pagans the power of God in these words: "He is Lord of
all, and all things are subject to His will, nor can anyone re-
sist His decree. If then ye will seek His help with your whole
heart ye shall perceive that His omnipotent power will not
fail you . . . Christ . . . is the strongest of the gods and
can aid those who hope in Him, in any way that He chooses.
. . . Worship the true God who rules all things in heaven and
earth, submit yourselves to Him and adore His almighty
power."[10]

From other Swedish converts come echoes of the same
familiar theme. An old woman declares, "The Lord, even
my Jesus Christ, is omnipotent, and if I continue to believe
in Him, He can give me health and everything that I need
according to His good pleasure." Another convert assures his
friends that "God can afford much help to those who place

[10] Rimbert, c. 19. Robinson's translation.

their hope in Him. For many of us have proved this to be the case on several occasions when in peril by sea or in other crises. . . . We have frequently proved that the help afforded by this God can be useful to us. . . . It is good for us to have the help of this God who is always, and under all circumstances, able and willing to succor those who cry to Him."[11]

Even pagan Swedes in a military emergency are willing to affirm that "the God of the Christians frequently helps those who cry to Him and His help is all powerful. Let us enquire whether He will be on our side, and let us with a willing mind promise offerings that will be agreeable to Him." And after casting lots which fell in their favor, they cry, "What have we now to fear or dread? Christ is with us . . . nothing can withstand us, nor shall we fail to secure certain victory, for we have the mightiest of the gods as our helper . . ." "When at length peace had been established between the two peoples [the Swedes and the inhabitants of Courland], the Swedes extolled with utmost zeal the omnipotence and glory of Christ our Lord and declared that he was greater than all other gods."[12] That Jesus Christ should play the rôle of a popular war-god may seem strange to modern minds; but in that time and place (as well as in others less remote) He was not known in any fashion that would make such a part uncongenial to Him.

Another familiar theme of Christian preaching was the doctrine that the pagan gods were not mere figments of the imagination; they were demons, and as such they must be renounced at baptism. Rimbert gives it as his own opinion that these gods are demons, and Herigar says to his people, "Your vows and sacrifices to idols are accursed by God. How long will ye serve devils and injure and impoverish yourselves by your useless vows?" And again, "Ye now understand that it is useless to seek for help from demons who cannot succor those who are in trouble."[18]

Both the dogma of God's omnipotence and the Christian

[11] Rimbert, cc. 20, 27.   [12] Ibid., c. 30.   [18] Ibid., c. 19.

conviction that heathen gods were demons find authoritative expression in the contemporary letter of Pope Nicholas I (864) addressed to Horic the Younger, King of the Danes. "Cease, therefore," he exhorts the monarch, "to worship idols, give up serving demons . . . adore the true God; recognize yourself as the servant of Him who alone is all-powerful, who holds everything in His hand, who is ineffable, immense, infinite, simple, immutable . . . immortal, all goodness, all pity, all holiness, who can aid you in this world and make you happy in the next."[14] Goodness, pity, and holiness, however, were attributes less familiar than omnipotence in most missionary preaching and still less congenial to the minds and hearts of Scandinavian converts.

While we have no examples on record of the Christian message as later proclaimed in Scandinavia, it is not difficult to learn from the sagas and other literature the form which Christianity took in its early days in that country and the aspects of the new religion which made the strongest popular appeal. These have been vividly described by Axel Olrik in his brilliant work *Viking Civilization*.

"We learn from many varied sources that Christ was regarded as the best helper in need. The tendency of the people to choose a lord according to their own best judgment aided the spread of Christianity. . . . God the Father disappears almost entirely; these warrior souls did not feel the need of clinging to a Father. The words 'God' and 'Christ' are synonymous. Christ created the world in days of old. He is the ruler of the heavens. . . . His suffering was completely incomprehensible to them; but His divine splendor as contrasted with men was the principle phase of the faith of the times. . . . We encounter a crude faith in the ruler of the heavens, fashioned after the image of earthly kings, with His citadel and His retinue. . . . This early Christianity wears a bright aspect, very different from the sense of an inescapable fate . . . that belonged to paganism. The mighty Christ, His victorious resurrection,

[14] *M. G. H. Epistolae*, vol. VI, no. 27, p. 293.

His bright kingdom of heaven, are the fundamental notes.
. . . Among all the Germanic peoples the foremost thought
seems to have been this: Christ is the mighty God of heaven,
with His retinue of apostles, while He wanders on earth, and
of angels after He had been restored to His heavenly stronghold. Perhaps this explains the readiness of men to enter
His service. . . . The belief in God's omnipotence, the
steadfastness with which the adherents of Christ went into
battle, full of trust in Him, is stated in all the sources as
being the strongest influence that weighted the scales on
the Christian side." [15]

As a final example may be cited the message of Otto of
Bamberg. During his two brief expeditions to Pomerania the
bishop spent little time in missionary preaching, for as we
have explained in an earlier chapter, his main purpose was
to organize the Church among a people who had at least
formally expressed their readiness to accept Christianity.
If, upon his approach, the members of a community agreed
to be baptized, he attempted no preaching at all but confined himself to brief instruction. Only if they declined the
offer of salvation did he address them as a persuasive messenger. We have therefore much more material for sum-
marizing his teaching than for describing his preaching.
And what few fragments of his public appeals are recorded
cannot be accepted as verbally genuine. But they serve at
least to remind us of what his closest followers and admirers
regarded as appropriate and probable.

To the people of Pyritz, for example, he declared, "We
have come a long way: it is for your salvation, your benefit,
and your happiness that we have made so great a journey.
For ye will be happy, safe, and blessed for evermore if ye
will acknowledge your Creator and will serve Him." [16] Aside
from instruction to those baptized or about to be baptized,
this brief message is practically all that can be gleaned from
the first missionary journey.

In the story of the second tour we find in an account of a

[15] Olrik, pp. 142–149.   [16] Herbordus, II, 15.

conference held at Usedom the arguments by which those who favored the acceptance of Christianity appealed to those who were still in doubt. As echoing the missionary message which they themselves had received from Otto and his followers their ideas are of value for our purposes. They "urged that when all the provinces belonging to the surrounding nations and the whole Roman world had submitted to the yoke of the faith, it would be the height of folly for them to be estranged, as an abortive offspring, from the womb of their sacred mother, the Church. They urged, too, that the God of the Christians deserved to be loved inasmuch as He had, during so many years, borne with their rebelliousness and had patiently waited for their conversion, and that they should fear lest, if they refused any longer to accept His yoke, they should incur the unbearable punishment of divine wrath." [17] This appeal to make haste and join the vast majority had been often used by earlier missionaries, and its effect would naturally tend to increase as the domain of heathenism rapidly narrowed with the passage of time.

In another account of the same conference we read that "the bishop on this occasion addressed to them a marvellous discourse and spoke of the coming of the Holy Spirit, the remission of sins, the various gifts of grace, the goodness of God and divine mercy, and preached unto them Jesus." And some months later at Stettin his preaching, we learn, was "concerning the judgment and compassion of God and the uncertainty of this present life and the continuance of things that are eternal." [18]

[17] Ebo, III, 6. Robinson's translation.
[18] Herbordus, III, 3, 18.

SUGGESTIONS FOR FURTHER READING

FOR those who wish to make a thorough study of the whole field, using the Latin sources and secondary works in English, French, and German, the bibliography will supply full details. For the general reader, however, the following suggestions will be more useful. Full titles, including place and date of publication, will be found in the bibliography.

For all the areas except Scotland and England, by all odds the most valuable work, which has brought me far more help than any other, is Hauck's *Kirchengeschichte Deutschlands*. The only English work covering all the fields is Robinson's *Conversion of Europe*, valuable as a handbook but not always thorough or reliable from the scholar's point of view. *The Cambridge Medieval History* is a monument of scholarship known to all.

Scotland: Skene, *Celtic Scotland*; Dowden, *Celtic Church in Scotland*; MacEwen, *History of the Church in Scotland*; Scott, *St. Ninian*; Adamnan's *Life of Columba*; Simpson, *The Historical St. Columba*; Duke, *The Columban Church.*

England: Bede's *Ecclesiastical History*, a fascinating and reliable source, available in King's or Sellar's translation. The notes in Plummer's Latin edition are of exceptional value. Howorth, *St. Augustine of Canterbury*; Browne, *Augustine and His Companions*; Mason, *The Mission of St. Augustine*; Barmby's translation of Gregory I's Letters; Browne, *Conversion of the Heptarchy*; Howorth, *Golden Days of the Early English Church*; Hunt, *The English Church, 597–1066*; Bright, *Early English Church History*; Hodgkin, *History of England to the Norman Conquest*; Oman, *England before the Norman Conquest.*

Columban: Jonas' *Life of Columban* and Walahfrid's *Life of Gall*; Metlake, *Life of St. Columban*; McCarthy, *Montalembert's St. Columban*; Holmes, *Origin and Development of the Christian Church in Gaul.*

Willibrord: Grieve, *Willibrord*, including a translation of Alcuin's Life of Willibrord.

Boniface: Willibald's *Life of Boniface*; Kylie, *English Correspondence of St. Boniface*; Browne, *Boniface of Crediton*, including a translation of most of his important letters.

Anskar: Robinson's translation of the Life by Rimbert.

Otto: Robinson's translation of the Lives by Ebo and Herbordus.

Sweden: Stomberg, *History of Sweden*; Hallendorff and Schück, *History of Sweden*; Wordsworth, *National Church of Sweden.*

Norway: Monsen's translation of the Heimskringla; Gjerset, *History of the Norwegian People*; Willson, *History of the Church in Norway.*

BIBLIOGRAPHY

BIBLIOGRAPHY

A. Sources

M. G. H. = *Monumenta Germaniae historica*
SS. = *Scriptores*
S. R. M. = *Scriptores rerum merovingicarum*

ADALBERTI, S., *Passio, M. G. H., SS.* XV, Pt. 2.
ADAM OF BREMEN, *Gesta Hammaburgensis ecclesiae pontificum, Script. rerum Germ.*, 3rd edit. ed. B. Schmeidler, Hanover, 1917.
ADAMNAN, *Vita Sancti Columbae*, edited and translated by W. Reeves in Historians of Scotland, vol. VI, Edinburgh, 1874.
ALCUIN, *Epistolae, M. G. H. Epistolae,* IV.
ALCUIN, *Vita Willibrordi, M. G. H., S. R. M.,* VII, ed. Levison.
ALTFRID, *Vita Liudgeri*, ed. W. Diekamp, Geschichtsquellen des Bisthums Münster, vol. IV, Münster, 1881.
AMANDI, *Vita, M. G. H., S. R. M.,* V, ed. B. Krusch.
ANDERSON, A. O., *Early Sources of Scottish History*, Edinburgh, 1922.
Annales Bertiniani, Script. rerum Germ., Hanover, 1883.
Annales Einhardi in *Annales regni Francorum, Script. rerum Germ.*, Hanover, 1905.
Annales Fuldenses, Script. rerum Germ., Hanover, 1891.
Annales Hildesheimenses, Script. rerum Germ., Hanover, 1878.
Annales Laureshamenses, M. G. H., SS. I.
Annales Laurissenses in *Annales regni Francorum, Script. rerum Germ.*, Hanover, 1905.
Annales Mettenses, Script. rerum Germ., Hanover, 1905.
BAEDAE VENERABILIS, *Opera historica*, edited and translated by J. E. King, Loeb Classical Library, London, 1930.
BAEDAE VENERABILIS, *Opera historica*, edited by C. Plummer, Oxford, 1896.
BAEDAE VENERABILIS, *Vita Cudbercti, Venerabilis Bedae opera historica minora*, ed. J. Stevenson, London, 1841.
BARMBY, J. See Nicene.
BEDE, THE VENERABLE, *Ecclesiastical History of England*, revised translation, edited by A. M. Sellar, London, 1912.
BÖHMER, J. E. *Regesta Imperii*, revised by E. Mühlbacher, Innsbruck, 1889.
Bonifatii et Lulli Epistolae, ed. M. Tangl, *Mon. Germ. Epist. Selectae* I, 1916.
BRUNO OF QUERFURT, *Vita Adalberti, M. G. H., SS.* IV.

Brunonis Vita, M. G. H., *SS*. XV, Pt. 2.

Burchardi Vita, M. G. H., *SS*. XV, Pt. 1.

CANAPARIUS, *Vita Adalberti*, M. G. H., *SS*. IV.

Capitulatio de partibus Saxoniae and *Capitulare Saxonicum* in M. G. H. *Leges*, Sect. II, vol. I.

Chronica Albrici, M. G. H., *SS*. XXIII.

Chronicon Montis Sereni, M. G. H., *SS*. XXIII.

COLUMBANUS, *Epistolae*, M. G. H. *Epistolae*, III, ed. W. Gundlach.

Cudbercti Vita, auctore anonymo, *Venerabilis Bedae opera historica minora*, ed. J. Stevenson, London, 1841.

EBO, *Vita Ottonis, Bibliotheca rerum Germanicarum*, vol. V, ed. P. Jaffé, Berlin, 1869.

EDDIUS STEPHANUS, *Vita Wilfrithi*, edited and translated by B. Colgrave, Cambridge, 1927.

EIGILIS, *Vita Sturmi*, M. G. H., *SS*. II.

EINHARDUS, *Vita Karoli Magni*, *Script. rerum Germ*., 6th edit., Hanover, 1911.

EKKEHARDUS, *Chronicon*, M. G. H., *SS*. VI.

EWALD AND HARTMANN (E. AND H.). See Gregorii.

FLORENTIUS WIGORNIENSIS (Florence of Worcester), *Chronicon, Monumenta historica Britannica*, 1848, vol. I.

FREDEGARIUS, *Chronicon*, M. G. H., *S. R. M.*, II.

Gregorii I Papae Registrum Epistolarum, M. G. H. *Epistolae*, II, ed. Ewald and Hartmann, 1891–99.

GREGORY OF TOURS, *Historia Francorum*, ed. H. Poupardin, Paris, 1913.

GREGORY OF TOURS, *History of the Franks*, translated by O. M. Dalton, Oxford, 1927.

GRIEVE, A., *Willibrord*, including translation of Alcuin's *Vita Willibrordi*, London, 1923.

GUILELMUS GEMETICENSIS (WILLIAM OF JUMIÈGES), *Gesta Normannorum ducum*, ed. J. Marx, Rouen and Paris, 1914.

HADDAN, A. W. AND STUBBS, W., *Councils and Ecclesiastical Documents relating to Great Britain and Ireland*, Oxford, 1869–1878.

HELMOLD, *Chronica Slavorum*, *Script. rerum Germ*., Hanover, 1868.

HERBORDUS, *Dialogus de Ottone, Bibliotheca rerum Germanicarum*, vol. V, ed. P. Jaffé, Berlin, 1869.

HOFMEISTER, A. See *Monachus Prieflingensis*.

JOCELINUS, *Vita Kentegerni*, edited and translated by A. P. Forbes in Historians of Scotland, vol. V, Edinburgh, 1874.

JONAS OF BOBBIO, *Life of St. Columban*, edited and translated by D. C. Munro, rev. ed., Philadelphia, 1895.

JONAS OF BOBBIO, *Vita Columbani*, M. G. H., *S. R. M.*, IV, ed. B. Krusch.

JOYNT, M. See Walahfrid.
KRUSCH, B. See Amandi and Jonas and Walahfrid.
KYLIE, E., *The English Correspondence of St. Boniface*, London, 1911.
LACOMBLET, T. J., *Urkundenbuch für die Geschichte des Niederrheins*, Düsseldorf, 1840.
Lebuini, Vita, M. G. H., SS. II.
LEVISON, W. See Alcuin, Willibald.
Liber Historiae Francorum, M. G. H., S. R. M., II.
Liber pontificalis, ed. L. Duchesne, Paris, 1886.
Leobae Vita, M. G. H., SS. XV. Pt. 1.
LIUDGER, *Vita Gregorii abbatis Traiectensis, M. G. H., SS.* XV, Pt. 1.
Liudgeri Vita. See Altfrid.
MIGNE (ED.), *Patrologia Latina.*
MONACHUS PRIEFLINGENSIS, *Vita Ottonis,* ed. A. Hofmeister, Griefswald, 1924.
Nicene and Post-Nicene Fathers, Second Series, New York, 1890–1898. Vols. XII and XIII include the works of Gregory the Great, translated and edited by James Barmby.
Norges Gamle Love, Christiania, 1846–95.
O'DONNELL, MANUS, *Life of Columcille,* edited and translated by A. O'Kelleher and G. Schoepperle, Urbana, Illinois, 1918.
Olaui Beati Passio et Miracula, ed. F. Metcalfe, Oxford, 1881.
OTLOH, *Vita Bonifatii, Script. rerum Germ.,* ed. Levison, 1905.
PARDESSUS, J. M., *Diplomata, chartae . . . ad res Gallo-Francic. spect.,* Paris, 1843, 1849.
PLUMMER, C., *Two of the Saxon Chronicles,* Oxford, 1892.
PLUMMER, C., *Vitae sanctorum Hiberniae,* Oxford, 1910.
Preussiches Urkundenbuch, Königsberg, 1882.
REEVES, W. See Adamnan.
Relatio de piis operibus Ottonis, M. G. H., SS. XV, Pt. 2.
RIMBERT, *Life of Anskar,* edited and translated by C. H. Robinson, London, 1921.
RIMBERT, *Vita Anskarii, Script. rerum Germ.,* ed. G. Waitz, Hanover, 1884.
ROBINSON, C. H., *The Life of Otto, Apostle of Pomerania,* by Ebo and Herbordus, London, 1920.
ROBINSON, C. H. See Rimbert.
ROBINSON, G. W. See Willibald.
SAXO GRAMMATICUS, *Gesta Danorum,* ed. A. Holder, Strasburg, 1898.
SCHMEIDLER, B. See Adam of Bremen.
Scriptores rerum Prussicarum, Leipzig, 1861.

SELLAR, A. M. See Bede.

SNORRE, STURLASON, *Heimskringla or Lives of the Norse Kings*, ed. by E. Monsen and translated into English with the assistance of A. H. Smith, Cambridge, 1932.

SNORRI, STURLUSON, *Heimskringla* (Nóregs Konunga Sǫgur), ed. F. Jónnson, Copenhagen, 1893–1900.

STEPHANUS. See Eddius.

STUBBS, *Registrum sacrum anglicanum*, 2nd ed., Oxford, 1897.

TANGL, M., *Briefe des hl. Bonifatius*, Leipzig, 1912.

THIETMARUS, *Chronicon, Script. rerum Germ.*, Hanover, 1889.

THOMAS OF ELMHAM, *Historia monasterii S. Augustini Cantuariensis*, ed. Charles Hardwick, London, 1858.

THORNE, GULIELMUS, *Chronica*, ed. R. Twysden in *Historiae Anglicanae Scriptores* X, London, 1652.

WALAHFRID, STRABO, *Life of St. Gall*, translated by Maud Joynt, London, 1927.

WALAHFRID, STRABO, *Vita Galli, M. G. H., S. R. M.*, IV, ed. B. Krusch.

WETTINUS, *Vita Galli, M. G. H., S. R. M.*, IV.

WIDUKINDUS, *Res gestae Saxonicae, Script. rerum Germ.*, Hanover, 1904.

Wigberti Vita, M. G. H., SS. XV, Pt. 1.

Willehadi Vita, M. G. H., SS. II.

WILLIAM OF JUMIÈGES. See *Guilelmus Gemeticensis*.

WILLIBALD, *Life of Boniface*, edited and translated by G. W. Robinson, Cambridge, U. S. A., 1916.

WILLIBALD, *Vita Bonifatii, Script. rerum Germ.*, ed. Levison, 1905.

Willibaldi et Winnebaldi Vitae, M. G. H., SS. XV, Pt. 1.

B. OTHER WORKS

ALLEN, C. F., *Histoire de Danemark*, translated from the Danish (7th edit.) by E. Beauvois, Copenhagen, 1878.

ARUP, E., *Danmarks Historie*, Copenhagen, 1925.

BASSENGE, E., *Die Sendung Augustins zur Bekehrung der Angelsachsen*, Leipzig, 1890.

BERLIÈRE, U., *L'ordre monastique des origines au douzième siècle*, Collection Pax, Paris-Lille, 1924.

BLANKE, F., *Die Entscheidungsjahre der Preussenmission (1206–1274)*, Zeitschrift für Kirchengeschichte, XLVII, 1928.

BLANKE, F., *Die Missionsmethode des Bischofs Christian von Preussen*, Altpreussische Forschungen, IV, 1927.

BOEHMER, H., *Zur Geschichte des Bonifatius*, Zeitschrift des Vereins für hessischen Geschichte und Landeskunde, L, 1917.

BRIGHT, W., *Chapters of Early English Church History*, 2nd edit., Oxford, 1888.

BRIL, L., *Les premiers temps du christianisme en Suède, Revue d'histoire ecclésiastique*, XII, 1911.

BROU, R. P., *St. Augustin de Canterbury et ses compagnons*, 3me édit., Paris, 1898.

BROWNE, G. F., *Alcuin of York*, London, 1908.

BROWNE, G. F., *Augustine and his Companions*, 2nd edit., London, 1897.

BROWNE, G. F., *Boniface of Crediton*, London, 1910.

BROWNE, G. F., *The Conversion of the Heptarchy*, London, 1896.

BUGGE, A., *Norges Historie*, I, Christiania, 1910–1912.

BURTON, J. H., *History of Scotland*, 2nd edit., Edinburgh, 1873.

BUSS, F. J., VON, *Winfrid-Bonifacius*, ed. Scherer, Graz, 1880.

CABROL, F., *L'Angleterre chrétienne avant les Normands*, 2me édit., Paris, 1909.

Cambridge Medieval History, New York, 1911–32.

CASPAR, E., *Hermann von Salza*, Tübingen, 1924.

COLLINS, W. E., *The Beginnings of English Christianity*, London, 1898.

COOK, A. S., *Augustine's Journey from Rome to Richborough*, Speculum, I, no. 4, Cambridge, U. S. A., 1926.

DAVID, P., *La Pologne et l'évangelisation de la Poméranie aux XIe et XIIe siècles*, Paris, 1928.

DAVIS, H. W. C., *Charlemagne*, London, 1899.

Dictionnaire de théologie catholique, Paris, 1903+.

DIEKAMP, W. See Altfrid.

DOWDEN, J., *The Celtic Church in Scotland*, London, 1894.

DUDDEN, F. H., *Gregory the Great*, London, 1905.

DUKE, J. A., *The Columban Church*, London, 1932.

DUNN, J. J., *Irish Monks on the Continent*, Cath. Univ. Bull. X, Washington, 1904.

Encyclopedia Britannica, 14th edit., 1929.

ESSEN, L. VAN DER, *Étude critique et littéraire sur les vitae des saints mérovingiens de l'ancienne Belgique*, Louvain, 1907.

FICKER AND HERMELINK, *Handbuch der Kirchengeschichte*, 2nd edit., ed. G. Krüger, Tübingen, 1929.

FIELD, J. E., *Saint Berin, the Apostle of Wessex*, London, 1902.

FINSTERWALDER, P. W., *Wege und Ziele der irischen und angelsächsischen Mission im fränkischen Reich*, Zeits. für Kirchengeschichte, XLVII.

FISCHER, O., *Das Legatenamt des Bonifatius*, Forschungen zur deutschen Geschichte, XXVI, 1886.

FLASKAMP, F., *Das hessische Missionswerk des hl. Bonifatius*, Duderstadt, 1926.

FLASKAMP, F., *Die Missionsmethode des hl. Bonifatius*, 2nd edit., Hildesheim, 1929.

FLASKAMP, F., *Suidbercht*, Duderstadt, 1930.

GJERSET, K., *History of the Norwegian People*, New York, 1915.

GOUGAUD, L., *Gaelic Pioneers of Christianity*, New York, 1923.

GOUGAUD, L., *Les Chrétientés celtiques*, 2me édit., Paris, 1911.

GOUGAUD, L., *Christianity in Celtic Lands*, London, 1932.

GOUGAUD, L., *L'oeuvre des Scotti dans l'Europe continentale*, Revue d'histoire ecclésiastique, 1908, pp. 261 f.

GOUGAUD, L., Review of W. D. Simpson's "The Historical St. Columba" in *Scottish Gaelic Studies*, vol. II, Pt. I, June, 1927.

GOYAU, G., *La politique missionaire de l'empereur Louis le Pieux*, Revue d'histoire des missions, VI, 1929.

HAHN, H., *Bonifaz und Lul*, Leipzig, 1883.

HALLENDORFF, C. AND A. SCHÜCK, *History of Sweden*, London, 1929.

HAUCK, A., *Kirchengeschichte Deutschlands*, 4th edit., Leipzig, 1904.

HEFELE, C. J., *Histoire des Conciles*, translated and edited by H. Leclercq, Paris, 1907–21.

HELVEG, L., *Den Dansker Historie*, Copenhagen, 1862.

HODGKIN, T., *History of England from the Earliest Times to the Norman Conquest*. (Political History of England, ed. Hunt and Poole, vol. I), London, 1906.

HOFMEISTER, A., *Zur Chronologie und Topographie der ersten Pommernfahrt Ottos von Bamberg*, Pommersche Jahrbücher, XXII, 1924.

HOLMES, T. S., *Origin and Development of the Christian Church in Gaul*, London, 1911.

HOWORTH, SIR HENRY H., *The Golden Days of the Early English Church*, London, 1917.

HOWORTH, SIR HENRY H., *St. Augustine of Canterbury*, New York, 1913.

HUNT, W., *The English Church* (597–1066), London, 1899.

HUTTON, W. H., *The Lives and Legends of the English Saints*, New York, 1903.

JAFFÉ, P. (ED.), *Regesta pontificum romanorum*, 2nd edit., revised by W. Wattenbach, Leipzig, 1885–88.

JUNG-DIEFENBACH, J., *Die Friesenbekehrung*, 1931.

JURITSCH, G., *Geschichte des Bischofs Otto*, Gotha, 1889.

KEYSER, R., *Den Norske Kirkes Historie under Katholicismen*, Christiania, 1856–58.

KNIGHT, G. A. F., *Archaeological Light on the Early Christianizing of Scotland*, London, 1933.

KONEN, W., *Die Heidenpredigt in der Germanenbekehrung*, Düsseldorf, 1909.

KÜMMEL, W., *Die Missionsmethode des Bischofs Otto von Bamberg*, Gütersloh, 1926.

KURTH, G., *St. Boniface*, Paris, 1902.

LARSON, L. M., *Canute the Great*, New York, 1912.

LAUX, J. J., *Der hl. Bonifatius*, Freiberg, i. B., 1922.

LAWLOR, H. C., *The Monastery of St. Mochaioi of Nendrum*, Belfast, 1925.

LAWLOR, H. J., *The Cathach of St. Columba*, Proc. Royal Irish Acad., vol. XXXIII, Sect. C, no. 11, Dublin, 1916.

LEACH, H. G., *Angevin Britain and Scandinavia*, Cambridge, U. S. A., 1921.

LEVISON, W., *Die echte und die verfälschte Gestalt von Rimberts Vita Anskarii*, Zeitschrift des Vereins für hamburgische Geschichte, XXIII, 1919.

LEVISON, W., *Die Iren und die fränkische Kirche*, Historische Zeitschrift, 109, 1912.

LEVISON, W., *Zur Würdigung von Rimberts Vita Anskarii*, Schriften des Vereins für schleswig-holsteinischen Kirchengeschichte, VIII, 1926.

LIGHTFOOT, J. B., *Leaders in the Northern Church*, London, 1890.

LOOFS, F., *Der Beiname des Apostels der Deutschen*, Zeitschrift für Kirchengeschichte, V, 1882.

McCARTHY, E. J., *Montalembert's Saint Columban*, St. Columban's, Nebraska, 1927.

MacEWEN, A. R., *A History of the Church in Scotland*, 2nd edit., London, 1915.

MACLEAR, G. F., *History of Christian Missions during the Middle Ages*, Cambridge, 1863.

MARTIN, E., *Saint Columban*, 2me édit., Paris, 1905.

MASCHKE, E., *Der deutsche Orden und die Preussen*, Berlin, 1928.

MASON, A. J., *The Mission of St. Augustine*, Cambridge, 1897.

MAURER, K., *Die Bekehrung des norwegischen Stammes zum Christentum*, Munich, 1855–6.

METLAKE, G. (J. J. LAUX), *The Life and Writings of St. Columban*, Philadelphia, 1914.

METZNER, E., *Beiträge zur Geschichte der Einführung des Christentums in Preussen*, Würzburger Dissertatio, 1906.

MOREAU, E. DE, *St. Amand*, Louvain, 1927.

MOREAU, E. DE, *St. Anschaire*, Louvain, 1930.

MÜHLBACHER, E., *Deutsche Geschichte unter den Karolingern*, Stuttgart, 1896.

OEHLER, M., *Geschichte des deutschen Ritter-Ordens*, Elbring, 1908.

OLRIK, AXEL, *Viking Civilization*, translated, New York, 1930.

OMAN, SIR CHARLES, *England before the Norman Conquest*, 6th edit., New York, 1925.

PIRENNE, H., *Histoire de Belgique*, Brussels, 1902.

PLUMMER, A., *The Churches in Britain before A.D. 1000*, London, 1911.

PONCELET, A., *Le "testament" de S. Willibrord*, Analect. Bolland., XXV, 1906.

PRUTZ, H., *Die geistlichen Ritterorden*, Berlin, 1908.

ROBINSON, C. H., *The Conversion of Europe*, London, 1917.

ROTH, W., *Die Dominikaner und Franziskaner im Deutschordensland Preussen*, Dissertatio, Königsberg, 1918.

SCHMIDLIN, J., *Katholische Missionsgeschichte*, 1924.

SCHNÜRER, G., *Kirche und Kultur im Mittelalter*, 2nd edit., Paderborn, 1924–9.

SCHUBERT, H. VON, *Ansgar und die Anfänge der schleswig-holsteinischen Kirchengeschichte*, Schriften des Vereins für schleswigholsteinischen Kirchengeschichte, II, 2, Kiel, 1901.

SCHUBERT, H. VON, *Geschichte der christlichen Kirche im Frühmittelalter*, Tübingen, 1917–21.

SCOTT, A. B., *The Pictish Nation*, Edinburgh, 1918.

SCOTT, A. B., *S. Ninian*, London, 1916.

SHAHAN, T. J., *St. Columbanus at Luxeuil*, American Catholic Quarterly, Jan., 1902.

SIMPSON, W. D., *The Historical St. Columba*, 2nd edit., Aberdeen, 1927.

SIMPSON, W. D., *On Certain Saints and Professor Watson*, Aberdeen, 1928.

SIMPSON, W. D., *St. Columba*, in Aberdeen University Review, vol. XV, 3, July, 1928.

SKENE, W. F., *Celtic Scotland*, Edinburgh, 1877.

STOMBERG, A. A., *A History of Sweden*, New York, 1931.

TARANGER, A., *Den Angelsaksiske Kirkes Indflydelse paaden Norske*, Christiania, 1890.

THOMPSON, J. W., *Feudal Germany*, Chicago, 1928.

VOIGT, H. G., *Brun von Querfurt und die Bedeutung seines Missionswerkes*, Altpreussische Monatschrift, XLV, 1908.

VOIGT, H. G., *Der Missionsversuch Adalberts von Prag in Preussen*, Altpreussische Monatschrift, XXXVIII, 1901.

WAGNER-SCHWERIN, R., *Die Wendenzeit*, Berlin, 1899.

WATSON, W. J., *Rejoinder*, in Aberdeen University Review, vol. XV, 3, July, 1928.

WATSON, W. J., *Review of W. D. Simpson's "The Historical St. Columba,"* in Aberdeen University Review, vol. XV, 2, March 1928.

WATTENBACH, W., *Deutschlands Geschichtsquellen im Mittelalter*, Stuttgart, 1904.

WATTENBACH, W., *Die Lebensbeschreibung des hl . . . Willehads*, Leipzig, 1888.

WEHRMANN, M., *Die Lehr-und Predigttätigkeit des Bischofs Otto von Bamberg in Pommern*, Baltische Studien, XXVI, 1924.

WIEDEMANN, H., *Die Sachsenbekehrung*, Münster-i. W., 1932.

WILLSON, T. B., *History of the Church and State in Norway from the Tenth to the Sixteenth Century*, Westminster, 1903.

WILSON, HENRY A., *The Calendar of St. Willibrord*, London, 1918.

WORDSWORTH, J., *The National Church of Sweden*, New York, 1911.

INDEX OF NAMES

INDEX OF NAMES

Names of authors and works are included only when
they occur in the main text